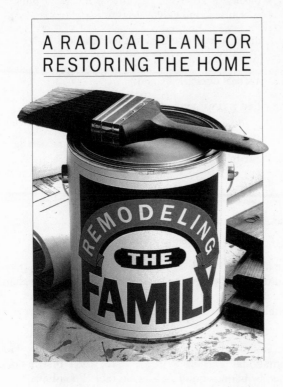

A RADICAL PLAN FOR
RESTORING THE HOME

REMODELING
THE
FAMILY

Bernie A. Schock, Ed.D.

Wolgemuth & Hyatt, Publishers, Inc.
Brentwood, Tennessee

The mission of Wolgemuth & Hyatt, Publishers, Inc. is to publish and distribute books that lead individuals toward:

- A personal faith in the one true God: Father, Son, and Holy Spirit;

- A lifestyle of practical discipleship; and

- A world view that is consistent with the historic, Christian faith.

Moreover, the Company endeavors to accomplish this mission at a reasonable profit and in a manner which glorifies God and serves His Kingdom.

Unless otherwise noted, all Scripture quotations are from the Holy Bible, New International Version © 1973, 1978, 1984 International Bible Society. Used by permission of Zondervan Bible Publishers.

Wolgemuth & Hyatt, Publishers, Inc.
1749 Mallory Lane, Suite 110, Brentwood, Tennessee 37027.
Printed in the United States of America.

Library of Congress Cataloging-in-Publication Data

Schock, Bernie, 1948–
    Remolding the home : a radical plan for restoring the family / Bernie A. Schock. — 1st ed.
        p.   cm.
    ISBN 0-943497-68-X : $14.95
    1. Family—Religious life. 2. Home schooling.   I. Title.
BV4526.2.S37 1989
261.8'3585—dc20   89-38489
                                                              CIP

To Cathy—for her willingness to love me and swim
against the cultural tide.

To my three sons—who significantly increase my joy and
my stress.

To my parents and extended family—who modeled intergenerational life without reading a book about it.

To my Lord—for guiding me in the path of genuine life
and freedom. To Him be the glory.

CONTENTS

Acknowledgments / *ix*

Introduction / *1*

PART ONE: INTELLECTUAL TRAINING

1. The Transformation of Schools / *7*

2. The Liabilities of Formal Schooling / *15*

3. Home-Centered Schooling / *23*

PART TWO: VOCATIONAL TRAINING

4. The Transformation of Work / *41*

5. Bringing Work Home / *53*

6. Family Work: Getting Your Hands Dirty / *63*

7. Children and Work / *71*

PART THREE: SOCIAL TRAINING

8. Socialization: The Loss of Community / *87*

9. Restoring Community: The Immediate Family / *97*

10. Restoring Community: The Extended Family / *113*

PART FOUR: SPIRITUAL TRAINING

11. Laying the Foundation / 127

12. Passing on the Faith / 137

PART FIVE: PHYSICAL TRAINING

13. Leisure in the Home / 153

14. Family Health / 169

PART SIX: CONCLUSION

15. You Can Remodel Your Family / 187

End Notes / 199

About the Author / 211

ACKNOWLEDGMENTS

Cathy and I frequently thank God for the solid founda-tion we received when we were babes in Christ. Campus Crusade for Christ was critical during our college years — the retreats, the conferences at Arrowhead Springs, and the staff pointed us to the path of life. The basics became solidified and expanded during our years at Dallas Seminary. We will always be thankful for an education that proclaimed (in word and in deed) the primacy of God's Word in answering man's needs. Many of the themes in this book have their roots in this early training.

Furthermore, I want to thank our friends, Rick and Kristi Casteel, and Steve and Suzi Kirby, as well as my brothers, Paul and Steve, for their advice, encouragement, disagree-ment, and love which have shaped the contents of this book. I also want to thank my editors Sally Rice and Sue Radosti, and my friend, Dick Sleeper, for his help in finding a pub-lisher.

Finally, I would like to thank the IBM Corporation. I can-not imagine writing a book without my personal computer.

INTRODUCTION

We have forfeited too much. The home has become a pit stop where people refuel for the "real" world. The result is a sense of alienation within the family. One dad lamented:

> I feel myself separated from my kids, like they are also being swept along a course from which there is no deviation. . . . I want to be close to them, to talk and kid with them. But they aren't too interested in me now and that is what hurts. I still have fun with the little ones, but the older they grow the farther they get from me. Something is wrong, something over which I have no control. . . . [But] I want to get back the connections to my family and my children.[1]

It hasn't always been this way. Puritan parents were intimately involved throughout their children's development:

> Fathers and mothers were expected to equip the children for reading the Bible and to catechize them faithfully. Fines were provided, though haphazardly enforced, for failure to instruct the children in Christian doctrine. . . . Puritans also strove to see their children "well-settled" in the world. To that end parents provided suitable apprenticeships, arranged for marriage partners from families of similar backgrounds (prospective spouses retained veto power), bestowed land, money, or tools as marriage gifts.[2]

1

But today, the family has vacated its role in training children. We depend on nursery schools to build kids' social skills, on schools to enrich their minds and prepare them for a vocation, on pastors to cultivate their spirituality, on health classes to teach them about their bodies. Stripped of its substance, home life has become so insipid that one study found that many children preferred T.V. to their fathers![3]

Most parents have lost confidence in nurturing their kids. A frequent refrain I hear from parents considering home education is: "I would love to—but I'm not a teacher." And the "experts"—teachers, psychiatrists, doctors, sociologists—have labored to convince us that we aren't qualified. (But what should we expect—their vocations depend on our deficiencies!)

But with all the professional help, are we any better off? It doesn't seem so—consider the problems:

- a fifty percent increase—up to twenty-two million—in the number of adult children living with their parents since 1970.[4]

- fifty percent more overweight children than twenty years ago.[5]

- an estimated twenty-three million illiterate adults, a number growing by 2.3 million yearly.[6]

- fifty percent of first-time marriages will end in divorce.[7]

- a tripling of teenage suicides over the last twenty years.[8]

- seventy percent of high school students admit that they have cheated in school.[9]

- sixty-nine percent of our never-married children will have engaged in sex by the time they are nineteen.[10]

The overwhelming problems demand radical thinking about the family. I use *radical* in two senses: first, "pertaining to root or origin." Our Biblical foundation provides the only untarnished guide to revive families. The prophet Malachi proclaimed that the Messiah would turn "the hearts of the fathers to their children, and the hearts of the children to their fathers" (see Malachi 4:1–6). Renewed hearts engender renewed homes.

However, our cultural roots can also instruct us — not because life was perfect in earlier America, but because they can clarify "what counts for us and what is special in our situation."[11] Unfortunately, modern man has become arrogant toward the past: "Each successive generation now feels it must start from scratch in making up the rules by which we play this game of life. . . . No information from the past about what is either helpful or hostile to human life is permitted to penetrate the present."[12]

Furthermore, a study of our history is important because many problems are rooted in the past. For example, our country's divorce rate has steadily increased since the 1860s — thus, we must retreat more than a century to understand its causes.

Second, I use *radical* in the sense of "favoring drastic reforms." As the crisis in the family mounts, we can't continue to assume that standard jobs are a necessity, that schools have the inalienable right to our kids, that the forty-hour work week is the Biblical model, that children can be nurtured on fifteen minutes of "quality" time each day.

Educator Allan Bloom has observed: "People are no longer raised to think they ought to regard marriage as the primary goal."[13] As a result, couples have "no common object, no common good," no shared vision of the role of the family. A friend of mine in an evangelical church was recently asked to substitute teach in a young couples' class. Class members wanted to talk about work, and their primary question was: "Whose work takes priority — husbands' or wives'?" They had no concept of the unity in God's design for marriage: "For this reason a man will leave his father and mother and be united to his wife, and they will become one flesh" (Genesis 2:24).

Husbands and wives need a common vision of the purpose and priority of the family. They need help in understanding and performing their God-given tasks in nurturing their children. This book will certainly not be the last word on family life. Parts of it may be hopelessly idealistic. But there is a desperate need to think Biblically, creatively, and drastically about our homes; they are quickly being relegated to bit parts in the twentieth-century drama.

PART ONE

INTELLECTUAL TRAINING

1

THE TRANSFORMATION OF SCHOOLS

In California, a textbook, may be rejected if it mentions a "birthday cake," thanks to the state's anti-sugar lobby.[1]

S chools are in trouble. Teachers don't want to teach—nearly half wish they had chosen another profession.[2] Students are unenthused about academics—friends and sports are their top school interests.[3] Scholastic Aptitude Test scores have decreased ten percent over the past twenty years.[4]

Whatever schools lacked in the past, it was not optimism. Horace Mann boasted that common schools could "hasten the millennium."[5] Another educator believed college instructors could impart more wisdom "than Solomon, Socrates, and Benjamin Franklin all together could give."[6] Americans differed on many issues but were united in their confidence that schools could redeem society.

[Schools] might be depended on to change immigrants into one hundred percent Americans [whatever *they* were];

freed slaves into middle-class Americans . . . ; racially prej-
udiced Southern [and Northern] whites into champions of
black equality; drunkards into teetotalers, and so on, virtu-
ally *ad infinitum*. Education was akin to being reborn from
sin into salvation.[7]

Though Americans obviously had overblown hopes,
schools have struggled to meet minimal expectations. A study
on the effects of a high school education found little evidence
that it "contributed to job competence or satisfaction, later
participation in civic and political activities, or life enjoyment."[8] What went wrong? Why have schools been so inef-
fective? Certain changes that have taken place in our culture
and in our schools contributed to the deficiencies.

Increased Time

The "good old days" of schooling weren't all that good.
Teachers were poorly trained. Discipline was harsh. There
were few good books. Kids' salvation came from a shorter
school year; as recently as the late nineteenth century, eight-
to fourteen-year-old children went to school only sixteen
weeks per year.[9] As the industrial revolution drew parents out
of the home, schools attempted to fill the void with longer
days and years. But schools could not replace the home.

Decreased Self-Esteem

Childhood is the time when children develop—or do not
develop—the sense of being able to do something well. Our
family grows pumpkins to sell door-to-door. Andrew, our middle son, has become a first-rate salesman. Customers are unable to resist his cheerful chatter as he bounds from house to
house. The confidence gained has transferred to other projects as well. When his Scout troop sold tickets to the Scout-
O-Rama, Andrew easily outsold the rest of his den.

But the expansion of schools has constricted kids' options for success.

> In the old days, if a child could not [succeed in school], all he had to do was to talk his father into letting him leave school, and usually his father was glad to have him home to feed pigs. Now we force the child to stick with it for at least ten years [years of continual failure for some] and in the end turn him out to fight his way against what the school has done for him. Even if they did fail [school] our grandfathers were successful at feeding the pigs. So many children in school today have had no successes.[10]

But why do so many students feel like failures today? Consider the difference between home and classroom learning:

> A father in a cornfield teaching his eight-year-old son how to plant maize finds it easy to create a situation that will accomplish this goal. It is more difficult when the child is with one teacher in a class of thirty children. . . . The larger the number of peers used for comparison, the less likely will a particular child conclude that he or she can master a particular talent.[11]

Sports have become ascendant in our culture largely because they provide one of the few alternate routes to achievement.

Decreased Parental Influence

The segregation of adults at work and children at school has weakened parental influence. As a result, many children turn elsewhere for help. In a study of thirty-six-hundred rural children, kids were asked how they coped with problems. Given fifty-four options, kids ranked "moms" thirty-first in their network of support. "Dads" fared even worse — a paltry forty-eighth! A child's peer group was one of the major props in these teens' lives.[12]

But the peer group offers only a temporary identity. Its preoccupation with appearance, music, sports, and entertainment does little to prepare teens for adult life; few will become fashion designers or rock stars or sports heroes. Without a variety of mature, adult models, many adolescents will be unequipped to make the transition from late childhood to self-sufficient young adulthood.

Decreased Skills

Many of us grew up in homes where domestic chores were handled by outsiders—repairmen, carpenters, plumbers, maids, and painters. But in early America, a person had to master a phenomenal number of skills to survive. A man:

> made soap and candles, thatched barns, built smokehouses.
> . . . He collected iron in the countryside and smelted it. He
> mended his children's shoes and his own. He built trundle
> beds, ox carts, sleighs, wagons, wagon wheels, and wheel
> spokes. He turned logs into boards and cut locust wood for
> picket fences. He made house frames, beams, mortised and
> pegged. With six men's help he raised the frames and built
> the houses.[13]

And he was capable of much, much more. But when a child's school day expanded, his practical skills contracted because schools emphasized book learning. Furthermore, specialization in the workplace eventually robbed parents of these talents. Most parents couldn't teach their child how to make soap if the fragrance of the world depended on it!

Hiring these expensive specialists increased our commitment to work—longer hours, second jobs, and mothers working. As a result, parents have less time for families, for reading, for reaching out to neighbors.

Increased Enrollment

The American belief that schools could regenerate society caused a zealous push for universal schooling—a goal largely achieved. But schooling for all has not been an unqualified good.

Decreased Quality

Earlier in this century, eight thousand part-time students who also worked part-time were asked if they would attend school full-time if they were compensated for their lost wages. Only sixteen said they would![14] What happens when those eight thousand students are forced to attend school? All of us know. We have agonized while teachers explained and re-explained concepts to uninterested students. We have been irritated by the disruptions of unruly students. We have been bored with textbooks that are not challenging. (One study concluded that textbooks are too simple for fifty percent of the students.[15]) Compulsory schooling impedes the quality of education.

The concern to educate children equally can handicap education in absurd ways. The 1980 California Education Code devoted forty-two pages to explaining the rules covering bilingual education, but only two pages to discussing the subjects to be taught in the classrooms.[16] In a midwestern city, one of the city's junior high schools had a nationally-recognized science program. But the district proposed dropping the program—simply because not all children in the district could participate! In one state, to "satisfy a powerful feminist lobby, a publisher made sure to include a photo of a female truck driver, only to find he had, literally, to stop the presses because of a complaint the female was wearing a pink (i.e., stereotypically feminine) T-shirt."[17] No wonder public education is distressed.

Finally, a fear of causing offense to certain students has diminished the quality of education. Confronted with pupils of varying ethnic, religious, and social backgrounds, teachers avoid controversial stands. They cling to a nebulous middle ground, decrying the "extremists on both sides." But "is there something evil, in all cases, in extreme ideas? This, clearly, is not so."[18] Wasn't Jesus an extremist? Weren't the revolutionary leaders extremists? Wasn't Martin Luther an extremist? As a result of not wanting to nettle non-Christians, our history has been taught with little mention of the profound influence of Christianity on our national life. The fear of the ACLU may be stronger than the commitment to truth.

Decreased Mixing of Ages

In 1850 there were eighty thousand public schools but only ninety thousand teachers![19] A shortage of teachers? No, most students attended one-room schools. But as school populations grew, classes were determined by the ages of the students.

Though separating kids into age-inclusive classrooms had benefits (e.g., teachers could specialize), the old system had benefits as well. First, in one-room schools older students tutored younger students. As a result, cooperation rather than competition pervaded the classroom.

Furthermore, students in one-room schools had to be treated as individuals — tenth-graders and first-graders could not share the same curriculum. Additionally, these individuals could progress at their own pace because they didn't have twenty to twenty-five of their peers to keep up with.

Finally, by blending the ages, kids maintained a knowledge of other-aged children. One of my younger brothers recently had his first child — a girl. When Lauren was about six months old, she began spending one morning each week in our home. At first, our youngest, Jered, didn't know how to relate to her; he had not grown up with younger siblings. When he held her, he was stiff and uncertain. When she grew restless, he didn't know how to entertain her. When she fussed, he became *very* anxious. But as his knowledge grew, he became confident and comfortable in her presence.

Increased Control

Early Americans migrated from countries where the state monopolized education, believing that the citizens were too ignorant to handle their own affairs. But our founders had a unique vision: they believed that people could govern themselves, and thus, educate their own children. The attitude toward schools and religion was similar — attend the school or church of your choice.

But the vision faltered. Eventually, public educators cornered the market and came to believe they were the only capable educators. Their attitudes parallel those of mental health experts during the 1930s and 1940s. Those committed individuals labored to raise money and develop new programs to improve the deplorable conditions in mental health institutions. But

> behind all these themes and concerns was the assumption that institutions needed to exist, that the people in them needed to be there, and that there was no alternative to institutional care. . . . From the vantage point of today, we know that this assumption is largely invalid.[20]

There are better ways to treat many of the mentally ill than to institutionalize them — are there equal or better ways to educate children?

Decreased Alternatives

Public schools were victorious when they convinced legislators to collect taxes to support their schools. Gradually, other alternatives dwindled as most parents were unable to pay taxes *and* support their private schools. As a result, "the public school system is probably the closest Americans have come toward creating an established church."[21]

But is a single educational system best for our country? What would happen if our nation had only one church? One political party? One manufacturer of goods? One employer?

I do not believe public schools should be abandoned or that home schooling is right for every family. But alternatives in education are essential to a healthy democracy.

Decreased Flexibility

My friend travels extensively for his job. When his kids became old enough to travel with him, he petitioned the school to excuse them periodically. He planned to make the trips educational by exploring museums, hiking on nature trails, touring historical sites. But the school had a limit — one week per year. My friend asked again, but the school wouldn't bend. At this point he decided to take his children out of the school and educate them at home.

The Pharisees had the same problem — their rigid application of the Law prevented them from seeing that "the Sabbath was made for man, not man for the Sabbath." They sought to murder Jesus for healing on their Sabbath! As schools have gained control of education, they have sometimes forgotten that their rules should serve children, not vice versa.

Conclusion

Public schools increasingly dominated the educational scene until recently. But today, in response to the problems in public education, there is a mushrooming number of private and home schools.

The following chapters will evaluate the deficiencies of public schools and point out how home schooling answers these shortcomings. As mentioned, parents have increasingly forfeited their role in training their children. Home schooling can reclaim lost ground.

2

THE LIABILITIES OF FORMAL SCHOOLING

[Classrooms are] neither harsh and punitive nor warm and joyful; [they] might be described most accurately as flat. A great deal of what goes on in classrooms is like painting by numbers.[1]

On the average, each high school counselor must advise about 320 students.[2]

Grant Colfax was home-educated prior to enrolling at Harvard University. The Harvard admissions director was astonished that Grant "really enjoyed the learning process" — his enthusiasm "was really a remarkable thing."[3] Remarkable? Aren't schools designed to nurture a love for learning? The remarkable thing is that educators spend over $200 billion yearly on education and often snuff out the desire to learn.

After reading an early draft of this chapter, I realized that I had made formal schooling sound like a trek through hell. If I wrote similarly on the deficiencies of children, no one would ever have a child. The evaluation would be warped because no child would have all of the shortcomings (though some parents may think otherwise!) — and the weaknesses would be balanced by strengths. It is the same with schools. No school (hopefully!) is as desperate as the sum of this evaluation. This analysis deals only with generalizations, of which there are many exceptions.

Teachers: Who Is Teaching?

Like Rodney Dangerfield, teachers complain of a lack of respect. But do most deserve it? On SAT scores, education majors ranked twenty-fourth out of twenty-eight categories.[4] In Houston, sixty-two percent of the teachers failed a standard reading test and forty-six percent flunked the math test. A former student at a major university reported that even though students were required to take elementary-level content courses, they still struggled.

> To pass the math course, we had to pass a twenty-question proficiency exam which was offered repeatedly throughout the semester and consisted of sixth grade math problems. . . . Only two of us in a class of forty plus college students passed the exam on the first try, and over half of the class had to take it three times. I have no reason to think my class was unusual.[5]

Similar observations led Emily Feistritzer, head of the National Center of Education Information, to conclude that over half of the teacher training programs are seriously deficient and should be shut down.[6]

Furthermore, the commitment to teaching is waning. In 1971 only thirteen percent of teachers said they would not choose teaching if they could choose again. By 1976 the negative responses had increased to nineteen percent; by 1981 it was thirty-six percent, and by 1983 it had ballooned to forty percent.[7] Though there are obviously gifted and dedicated teachers, many appear to be only marginally competent and marginally committed to teaching our kids.

The Curriculum: What Is Taught?

Educator Neil Postman believes that his profession has lost sight of worthwhile goals:

> It is as if we are driving a multimillion dollar sports car, screaming, "Faster! Faster!" while peering fixedly into the rearview mirror. . . . We have paid almost exclusive attention to the car, equipping it with all sorts of fantastic gadgets . . . but we seem to have forgotten where we wanted to go in it.[8]

Educators' myopia has caused schools to stress the trivial—they don't want to change the world or put an end to poverty or discover how to use the wisdom of the elderly. They simply want to improve the test scores of children.

When wisdom is not the goal of education, students are impoverished: "A highly trained computer specialist need not have had any more learning about morals, politics, or religion than the most ignorant of persons."[9]

The curriculum of public education is not only shallow, but also unbalanced. Eda LeShan returned to her alma mater and found that even though millions had been spent on new buildings, the school of music was still housed in "a little gray frame house" that had been "tiny and ramshackle when [she] had been at school" but "seemed only more so now."[10]

Art and music programs are not priorities. Parents seldom meet with an art or music teacher. Their programs are axed first when budgets tighten. Why do we place a lesser value on creative abilities?

One of our boys went through a time when school work was agony—pencils flew through the air, fists pounded on the table, tears streamed down his face. School was a battle, ex-

cept during art. As a partial solution, we freed more of his time
to paint and draw. In a formal school, teachers can seldom adjust the curriculum to meet the varying interests of kids. Future
artists and chemists spend equal time in each subject. As a student I studied math endlessly—geometry, trigonometry, calcu-
lus. But what math do I use? I add and subtract, divide and
multiply, work fractions and calculate percentages. The math
that I presently use I was adept at in junior high. Though solv-
ing math problems certainly contributed to an ability to think
and analyze, I would gladly trade a few of those courses for ones
in woodworking, painting, or piano.

The Methodology: How Is It Taught?

W. R. Wees has aptly defined most schoolroom learning as
"telling" and "remembering." Teachers tell, students remember.

Telling

Passivity reigns in the classroom primarily because teachers monopolize the learning process. One study found that
55% of elementary students reported making *no* choices in
what they did in class. At the secondary level, when kids
should be progressing toward independence, nearly 70% were
uninvolved in classroom decisions![11] Wees concluded: "If you
don't let my kids speak their minds, they'll have no minds to
speak of."[12]

Teachers frequently complain about the trivial questions
that students ask: "When is it due?" "Should we type it?"
"Will you count off for misspelled words?" There will be no
enthusiasm for learning until students are brought into a
more active role.

Remembering

Our family spends several weeks each year in South
Dakota's Black Hills. Recently an adult asked how we enter-

tained the kids for that length of time. But young children are natural learners; they will spend hours studying the bugs sheltered beneath rocks. They will collect pine cones or deer bones or rocks or flowers.

So what steals kids' joy in learning? One problem is the overuse of memorization as a method of instruction. Thus, geography becomes "a list of names and places; history a list of events, dates, and names of people"; biology is the number of bones in the body, the names of the muscles, the placement of the organs.[13] But seldom are students led to marvel at the body's wonders — skin that thickens to protect from tearing; bones that are as strong as steel but self-repairing; a sense of touch that can discern the difference between a smooth pane of glass and one etched with lines only $\frac{1}{2500}$ of an inch deep.

Because memorizing is boring, schools use competition to put dazzle into drab subjects. Today, there are national competitions for "Number One *Math*lete," a U.S. Academic Decathlon, a National Academic Championship, a National Academic Super Bowl.[14]

One mother was shocked by the profusion of prizes that her triplets earned during *the first two weeks* of first grade:

> one candy bar, one peanut-butter-and-chocolate-chip cookie, two bags of popcorn, two "Very Important Person" badges, three "Constitutional Knowledge" stickers, one "I Know the Alphabet" award, two drawing prizes, thirty-one Nature Trail tickets, nine Lincoln play dollars, several music awards, some library awards, "Neater Eater" awards, playground-behavior awards and innumerable Scratch-N-Sniff stickers, stamps, stars, and smile faces. What an introduction to the Lincoln School's positive-incentive program![15]

Though her school was an extreme, all schools use awards to counter the disinterest of students. We must share her concern for the children trained by this system:

[They] will . . . suffer if they don't discover for themselves that they can gain the pleasure of health and strength from exercise, the joy of music from songs, the power of mathematics from counting, and all of human wisdom from reading. I'm going to do my utmost to teach my children about these rewards.[16]

The Students: How Are They Affected?

Fear

I am in agony—it is near the end of the semester, and I have a class that I have attended only once. I know that it will be nearly impossible to complete the classwork, but I hope to arrange something with the professor. But unbelievably, I can't find his office or anyone who knows where it is. I begin to panic—racing down the halls, frantically looking in classroom after classroom, hoping to unveil this hidden professor. I keep searching and searching, knowing that if I can't uncover him, I will fail the class. My salvation arrives when I awake from my dream.

That frequent dream has its roots in my school days:

- My thundering, eighth-grade math teacher who demanded perfection and publicly chastised imperfection.

- Another teacher who tore into impolite students who raised their hand while she was speaking.

- A second-grade teacher who threatened her students with: "These tardies will go on your permanent record and you will never be able to get a job."

Former educator and author John Holt taught in a progressive school that didn't give grades. When he asked a class how they would feel if they couldn't answer a teacher's question, one boy said "gulp." Holt wanted to know why they felt "gulpish." They explained that "they were afraid of failing, afraid of being kept back, afraid of being called stupid, afraid of feeling themselves stupid." Holt's conclusion was that "even in the kindest and gentlest of schools, children are afraid, many of them a great deal of the time, some of them almost all the time."[17]

Indifference

A student interested in academics may feel like an alien in the classroom. When John Goodlad, former dean of the Graduate School of Education at U.C.L.A., conducted a survey of high school students, he found that their favorite part of school was "my friends." "Nothing" (eight percent) outranked "classes I'm taking" (seven percent)! Goodlad concluded: "The students we studied were not fired up over their teachers, the classes they were taking, or the curriculum."[18]

Student indifference may explain why ninety percent of a class of college freshmen said they would skip the rest of college in exchange for a diploma.[19] I was like the ninety percent, until one day a rather exasperated seminary professor — we had probably asked one of those inane questions like, "Will we have to know this for the test?" — rebuked us, saying: "Listen, men, when you get out of here no church is going to ask what you made in this class. What they will want to know is whether you can apply your theology to your life and ministry." That statement turned me around — I began to study to learn, rather than make high marks.

Conclusion

Americans have depended on money to solve problems. Since 1949 we have *quadrupled* our per pupil spending (in dollars adjusted for inflation).[20] But are our students four times more competent? No one believes they are. A recent report by the Committee for Economic Development concluded that fifty percent of high school graduates cannot read well enough to handle "moderately complicated tasks."[21] Incredibly, teachers' unions, educators, and many politicians claim that spending more money will cure many of our educational ills.

Can public schooling be reformed? Probably. Must all Christians dedicate themselves to that task? Certainly not. As pointed out earlier, a democratic society is strengthened by diversity.

My concern is to help parents fulfill their God-given role in training their children. Home schooling can help them accomplish that goal.

3

HOME-CENTERED SCHOOLING

God, guard me from those thoughts
men think
In the mind alone;
He that sings a lasting song
Thinks in marrow-bone.

William Yeats

S uppose a stranger came to your door and asked: "Could I have your child for thirty hours a week for the next forty weeks?" We would be stunned, and yet it is not unlike what schools ask of parents. We know little about the what or the who or the how of teaching. Yet we entrust our kids to this unknown system for over thirteen thousand hours during their childhood!

Moses instructed the Israelites to share all of life with their children: "when you sit at home and when you walk along the road, when you lie down and when you get up" (Deuteronomy 6:7). Home schooling allows parents to be involved in their kids' education—a practice foreign to most homes. "People sup together, play together, travel together, but they do not think together. Hardly any homes have any intellectual life whatsoever."[1]

The Assets of Home Schooling

Home schooling is not the perfect educational solution — there are no perfect solutions in an imperfect world. Nor is home schooling the only alternative for committed parents. But it may be the best choice for many families.

The Teachers

"What can I offer?" Home school teachers have the greatest asset — time. Child development specialist David Elkind concludes that there are three variables that affect learning — the teacher, the student, and the amount of time they spend together.[2] How much one-on-one time does a student have with a classroom teacher? Even if a teacher broke the day into individualized segments, each child would get about ten minutes. But it is obviously far less. A child probably receives one or two minutes *daily*, or four or five hours *yearly*. On the other hand, a home taught child enjoys that much time each week.

Furthermore, a home educator can build on what she knows about her kids; a classroom teacher starts over each year. Our son, Andrew, loves to smash, squash, unravel, dismember, punch, poke, and drown things. When this trait surfaced he would frequently, and sheepishly, exclaim, "Gee, I didn't know that would happen!" At first, we were worried that we had a naughty boy. But we came to realize that he was not acting mischievously; he was simply curious. We doubt many schoolteachers would have time to understand our creative (or is it destructive?) child.

One child is ready to read at four; another isn't ready until seven. One third-grade child loves to write poems; another is wearied by having to write a single sentence. One child loves to explore new topics; another likes to spend months on the same one. One five-year-old can sit quietly listening to a story; another couldn't sit quietly if you strapped him in a chair and taped his mouth shut. Some interpreters believe that the admonition in Proverbs to "train a child in the way he should go" (Proverbs 22:6) is a call to adapt our training to the particular bent or nature of the child. It could then be translated, "train up a child in his unique way." Parents, much more than a classroom teacher, are capable of discerning their child's individuality.

"Am I qualified?" Many parents fear that they are not qualified to teach their children. But expertise develops through experience. In at least five states, a teacher needs no degree in history to be a history teacher.[3] Furthermore, literacy programs use high school graduates to tutor other adults. You may not be the greatest teacher initially, but with time and commitment, you can become an accomplished instructor.

One of the most critical factors in being a successful teacher is understanding child development. But most college curriculums don't emphasize this. Checking the catalogue of a local college I found that courses on instructional content outnumber courses on child development a whopping five to one. As a result, many parents have read more books on child behavior than schoolroom teachers have read.

Finally, children don't need someone with every answer; they simply need a model of an avid learner. Are you curious about your world? Do you have an appetite for books? What is critical is your I.Q. — your Inquisitive Quotient!

"Could I handle the pressure?" One mother explained: "I am a better mother when I get away from my kids during the day. I just about die in the summer when I am with them all day long." Is that the case? Are there mothers who would not be good mothers if their kids were home all day? I wonder.

There are many factors that effect the decision of whether to home school or not — how helpful will dad be?

Can mom give up her income? Is there a home schoolers' support group? But laying aside those factors, there are still some who question whether they could handle the task of home schooling.

Cathy's testimony is that being a home educator is not like a daily romp through Disney World. In fact, at its worst, she finds it more like a journey through Dante's Inferno! But the hardships have forced her to depend on God's strength — learning how to be patient with a child whose memory is as fleeting as a spring snow; how to forbear when a boy repeatedly solves conflicts with his fists; how to be kind to children who express little appreciation. Though she has frequently faltered, her weakness has led to a greater strength:

> But [Jesus] said to me, "My grace is sufficient for you, for my power is made perfect in weakness." Therefore I will boast all the more gladly about my weaknesses, so that Christ's power may rest on me. That is why, for Christ's sake, I delight in weaknesses, in insults, in hardships, in persecutions, in difficulties. For when I am weak, then I am strong. (2 Corinthians 12:9, 10)

Is home schooling too difficult for *some* mothers? No, it is too difficult for *all* mothers. But it can be the means of learning how to depend on God's power.

The Curriculum: What Do I Teach?

It is a truism to say that the Bible must form the backbone of our teaching. But our aim is not merely an accumulation of Biblical facts. In the Old Testament verbs for *knowing* are paralleled with verbs for *doing*. The New Testament is similar — Paul prayed that the Philippians' love would "abound more and more in knowledge" so that they would be able to "discern what is best and may be pure and blameless until the day of Christ" (see Philippians 1:9f). The best way to prepare our children for the future is to transmit a knowl-edge of how to live.

> Wisdom is a shelter as money is a shelter, but the advan-tage of knowledge is this: that wisdom preserves the life of its possessor. (Ecclesiastes 7:12)

Informal education. Does this sound familiar:
"I want that!"
"No, I want it!"
"But I had it first!"
"Ooooh, no! I had it sitting right here in my pile!"
"You give it to me or I'll sit on you!"
"You do and I'll tell Mom!"

The joys of children playing together! In the midst of their tussles, it is hard to remember that play is crucial to their development—teaching them how to compromise, lis-ten, criticize, understand, negotiate, and make peace. Thus, a home school curriculum can include play as an integral part of education.

Furthermore, other forms of informal education can con-tribute to the training of our children. Growing pumpkins to sell can teach kids about plant life, about the rewards of hard work, and about the joy of giving (when a young boy does not have enough money to buy a pumpkin). Or a home school curriculum can include visiting a shut-in, opening your home to a troubled teen, working around the home, preparing a meal for a sick family. Home schools can prepare children for the diversity of life's experiences without the kids even know-ing class is in session!

Formal education. But experience alone is an insufficient tutor. Before Jesus commissioned the Seventy to preach in Israel's cities, they were required to sit through Ministry 101. The course taught them how to handle rejection, what to take with them, what to expect. After their task was complete, Jesus brought them back into the classroom for debriefing. Educator Seymour Sarason explains: "In and of itself, doing can be a mindless affair. To glorify experience . . . is to devalue subject matter and to shortchange the individual in terms of understanding and coping with the world."[4]

The most effective curriculum, then, is one that unites subject matter with experience. For example, writing can include a letter to an out-of-town grandparent. A study of weeds can be combined with back yard gardening. A study of pollution might lead to an afternoon of cleaning up a local beach. A study of child development might be completed by babysitting. Or a study of finances can be coupled with placing a child on a personal budget. A whole curriculum includes leg work and book work — neither is expendable.

Choosing a curriculum. So what should you use in your day-to-day teaching? Public school books if they are available? One of the Christian curriculums from Abeka or ACE? Dr. Larry Arnoldsen, Professor of Education at Brigham Young University explained his choice: "Conventional curriculums should be set aside in favor of learner interests."[5]

But can our children survive without computer classes and science labs and foreign language study? During World War II, the best recruits of the Canadian Navy were farm boys. These were men whose "experience with bodies of water had been limited to the dug-out pond behind the barn."[6] But they knew how to learn and could use their creativity to solve problems. Thus, as Arnoldsen explains, we should not be concerned about mirroring the curriculum of schools: "I am not worried about the learner not learning what he needs to. The most important learning and outcome is how to learn, skills of learning."[7]

But be careful. Children's learning needs boundaries. If we give them absolute choice, they will ignore math or writing. They will listen to music rather than compose their own. They will draw in coloring books rather than create an original painting. However, within appropriate guidelines, children can make their own choices.

When we follow the interests of children, it allows them to relax in a subject — something that is nearly impossible in a traditional curriculum. One researcher discovered that in a high school science book students are confronted with seven to ten new concepts each page — or 2,400 to 3,000 yearly.[8] Thus, during a 180-day school year, the teacher would have only one or two minutes to explain each concept!

A few years ago, our family found letters that my dad had written during World War II. The boys were fascinated with them and later invited their grandpa over for questioning. Nathan, who was a sixth grader, became captivated and read twenty-five to thirty World War II books during the next few months. We occasionally recommended books that would broaden his understanding (e.g., Corrie ten Boom's, *The Hiding Place*). Another time, our boys became interested in fish. We read books about fish and the fishing industry. We drew fish. We dissected fish. We went fishing and cooked our catch. We visited a hatchery to see how fish are raised. Their enthusiasm mushroomed as their understanding grew. Kids' learning is most effective and enjoyable when it is concentrated.

Finally, there may be advantages to purchasing a comprehensive curriculum. First of all, it contains a common body of knowledge, particularly in literature and history, that helps a person relate to and understand our culture. Furthermore, a prepared curriculum lends security to nervous beginners (don't worry — we were all insecure when we started!). But keep in mind that the "traditional conception of curriculum gives far more direction and purpose to teachers than it does to the students."[9] Thus, use it as a guide and a base — but don't stick slavishly to it as schoolteachers are required to do. Explore your children's interests.

Readin' an' writin'. Most educators recognize that reading and writing are the cornerstone to a child's education. But most schools are not doing an adequate job in teaching these subjects.

Reading is normally taught by using basal readers rather than classic children's literature. This astounds one educator: "Is it possible that America's reading teachers think a controlled vocabulary 'developed' by pedestrian writers can compete with the works of the Brothers Grimm, Hans Christian Andersen, L. Frank Baum, or the myths of many lands? Stories about Dick and Jane cannot compete. In one study, those who were trained by 'real' books were later described as 'superior writers' and 'independent thinkers.' "[10]

Furthermore, reading of any kind is not accented in most schools. One national study found that elementary students spend about five percent of their class time reading, while junior and senior highers spend less than three percent of their school day reading![11] Thus, part of the Schock's "formal" education includes reading during afternoon rest and prior to bedtime.

Formal schools are also deficient in teaching the craft of writing. A group of composition teachers analyzed how to strengthen writing skills in students. They concluded that schools had hindered their own writing: "isolated skills [spelling, diagramming sentences, grammar, punctuation, and handwriting] had nothing to do with how we wrote or how we had learned to write. In truth, our own teachers' methods had had little positive effect — and much negative effect — on our writing."[12] Where did their writing blossom? Outside the classroom! They penned journals and diaries, letters, short stories, cartoons, poetry, plays, skits, essays. Following their advice, Cathy and I spend little time teaching language skills. We simply free our kids to write.

The Methodology: How Do I Teach?

An educator observed two methods of teaching kids about crystals. The first teacher defined crystals and explained how to make them. Then the children made crystals.

A second teacher exposed the wonder of crystal formation:

It was as much magic to me as to the kids; so we used it like a cooking activity. I told them that we didn't know why it happened, but they got the idea that when some things mix together, sometimes something extraordinary happens.[13]

This initial experiment inspired a bevy of experiments initiated by the children. They tried all sorts of weird concoctions, wanting to see what the mixtures would produce. (Fortunately, there were no explosions!)

How did the two methods differ? The first was deductive — the students were told what to do. When the task was completed, so was the kids' activity. The second was inductive — teachers and students were co-participants in learning.

Thus, our methodology should draw kids into the learning process. Daily, we are confronted with the unknown. What kind of bug is that? Why do leaves change color in the fall? Why didn't the French stand up to the Nazis prior to World War II? It is those questions — and the joint pursuit of answers — that should dominate our approach to teaching.

Our aim in education is not so much a body of facts but "a habit of mind." David Elkind reflected:

Parents who love learning will create a stimulating environment for children, which is far more beneficial to them than specific instruction. Parents who fill the house with books, paintings and music, who have interesting friends and discussions, who are curious and ask questions, provide young children with all the intellectual stimulation they need. In such an environment, formal instruction would be like ordering a hamburger at a four-star restaurant.[14]

The Students: How Will My Children Benefit?

Unhurried childhood. Andrew and Jered are early risers. When they awaken they crawl into our bed for a few minutes of cuddling. The radio is turned on, we spend time chatting about the coming day. Soon, Nathan drags in, heavy with sleep. By this time the other two are ready to play, so Nathan takes their place in bed. We eat breakfast about thirty minutes later, then pray about the day's events. Next, the boys get dressed, do a few morning chores and we begin school about 9:30.

But imagine what life could be like if they attended a formal school . . .

RINGGGGGGGGGGGGGGGGGGGGGGGGGGGG!

The alarm jostles me out of my last minutes of sleep. I jump out of bed and shout to the kids: "Time to get up and get moving! You don't want to be late for school."

I stumble to the kitchen and begin to fry some eggs while Cathy is busy making beds and dressing. Breakfast is almost ready as the first boy arrives in the kitchen.

"Good morning, Andrew. Where's the chart that you made for your health class? You don't want to forget it."

"Oh, it's in my room somewhere, Dad."

"Well, you better get it and put it by the back door."

I recognize that the basement—where Nathan sleeps—is dark and quiet. "Nathan, are you up yet? Better get moving."

When I serve breakfast, Andrew is the only one there. Nathan lingers downstairs and Jered agonizes over what shirt to wear. Eventually, Nathan joins us to gobble down his food, but Jered doesn't make it before his ride arrives. Cathy fixes him a piece of peanut butter toast to eat in the car.

Andrew's ride arrives, and he is nearly in the car before I notice that he doesn't have his chart.

"Andrew! You've forgotten your chart!" He hears me and races back into the house but is unable to locate it. "Dad, I've just got to find that chart. Mrs. Smith was really mad at the kids who forgot theirs yesterday."

I am getting exasperated with my forgetful son and bellow: "Andrew, I warned you earlier to locate that chart. Can't you ever remember what you are supposed to do?!"

His ride is honking, his dad is upset with him, and he is worried about producing a chart for Mrs. Smith. He leaves for school in a turmoil—with no chart.

Nathan comes upstairs again. He is wearing his favorite shirt—for the third day in a row. Cathy instructs him to change the shirt before he goes to school.

"But Mom, there isn't another decent shirt in my drawer. I'm not going to school wearing something weird."

"I'm sorry, Nathan, but you can't wear a dirty shirt."

Nathan stomps downstairs, changes shirts, and stomps out the door to meet his ride.

Glenn Latham, an education professor at Utah State University, estimates that schools waste over fifty percent of the school-day.[15] In home schooling, a child's work can be accomplished in much less time, thus giving a child a slower, less-pressured lifestyle.

Protected childhood. Young children need to be sheltered because their values are unstable until the late grade-school years. Dr Raymond Moore, after an extensive review of educational research, concluded:

> To send [your children] *unnecessarily* to out-of-home care during the first eight years or so before their habits and manners and values are well-established will generally dilute and pervert your efforts toward building a positive sociability. This in turn will make your children less secure, more peer dependent, more prone to anxiety, frustration, and learning failure.[16]

While most schooled children worry about matching the clothing, hairstyle, and music tastes of their friends, most home educated kids are less concerned about what is "in." Our boys, for example, enjoy dressing well, but don't feel compelled to dress like their peers.

The Length of Home Schooling

During the 1960s, Benjamin Bloom became famous for his childhood research. He concluded that a child's personality is

indelibly stamped during the early years. Bloom's findings
have led many parents to believe they don't "have to worry
about how much time they spend with their [older] kids, how
much they supervise their activities, how carefully they steer
them in one direction or another."[17] More recent research,
however, has found that the early years have been grossly
overemphasized. One study indicated, as might be expected,
that kids with working moms have greater difficulty in school.
But the study also found that *older* children are affected *more*
by their mothers' absence than younger ones![18]

Because experiences throughout life shape development,
our older kids need us too. Andrew decided to play on a
YMCA basketball team, and I volunteered to coach. During
the season, one of the boys became hostile toward Andrew —
an attitude that was quickly grasped by other team members.
My initial reaction was a strong desire to break the boy's
neck! But as Cathy and I investigated the conflict, we discovered that this boy's hostility toward Andrew was not unique;
it frequently erupted at school and at home. Over the next
few weeks we prayed with Andrew for this troubled boy. As a
result of gaining an adult perspective, our son wasn't discouraged by the ostracism of some of his teammates. Availability
as Andrew's coach made it possible to help him.

However, when kids attend school all day and play on
soccer teams after school and sleep at a friend's house on
Friday night and participate in church activities three times a
week, their burdens are not known by their parents. When
they do share a few minutes together, fatigue or indifference
may hinder communication.

Furthermore, long-term home schooling may be wise because of the ambience of secondary schools. A study conducted at the University of Michigan found that students had
less freedom in junior high than in grade school. The study
also observed that junior high teachers were "more sarcastic
and less supportive" than elementary teachers who were described as "consistently warmer."[19] Another national study

found that parents, students, and teachers all gave the upper grades lower ratings.[20]

Finally, we have been encouraged to extend home schooling because our children are allowed to attend our public schools part-time. They are able to participate in areas we lack the skills or the equipment — band, athletics, typing, and science.

The Liabilities of Home Schooling

The Teachers

Work outside the home can be enticing as the wife of a medical student found when she began teaching:

> My days were full and rewarding. I enjoyed my work immensely, and my students affirmed me most of the time. Moreover, I had excellent rapport with my colleagues and grew intellectually from this experience.

> In addition, the salary I earned financed lunches out with friends, lovely clothes, and vacations with Thomas. No longer was I an intern's depressed wife, mother of one child, who had little to say when the other doctors' wives asked that powerful question: "What do you do?" Instead, as a college instructor, I had status among the other interns and their wives, and this was no small sop.[21]

It is not easy for moms to become home educators. It involves financial, social, vocational, and emotional sacrifices. The rewards of home education are less tangible, more long term. As a result, a mother must approach home schooling cautiously, counting the cost.

Husbands, if you want your children taught at home, then you will have to uphold your wife. With few available neighbors, with extended family in distant cities, with friends employed during the day, a stay-at-home mom has lost most of her daily support. After five years of teaching three active, unpredictable boys, I noticed that Cathy was growing increasingly exhausted. She could identify with a pediatrician's advice to a new mother:

Mother: "When should I put my children to bed?"

Doctor: "When you still have the strength!"

It was time for us to pray and evaluate. Should we continue?

Our first conclusion was to continue, but we knew that Cathy needed bolstering. As a result, I altered and shortened my schedule to start earlier and end by mid-afternoon. However, few husbands have the flexibility that I have as a writer, but there are other ways to help. You can help with housework in the evenings; gather resources at the library; organize a reading time after dinner; find a college student who will exchange tutoring for room and board; assist your wife in planning and evaluating; let her sleep in on Saturdays; hire someone to help with the cleaning or cooking; conduct a science class in the evenings. Use your creativity. There are hundreds of ways you can help.

The Curriculum

Cathy's exhaustion came, in part, from trying to fill gaps that neither she nor I could fill. But God never intended us to fulfill all of our kids' needs. Paul told the Colossians that body growth comes from two sources: from the "Head" — Jesus Christ — and from the "ligaments and sinews" — the members of Christ's body. Cathy and I may be ligaments, but our boys also need sinews. As a result, we have become aggressive in finding ways to complement our home school curriculum.

Our home school association has begun a learning cooperative that allows families to share their skills and knowledge with other home schoolers. This past year, our co-op offered a tour of the historical sites in the city. There were classes in small engine repair, music appreciation, writing, and physical education. The cooperative has broadened our boys' education, while easing some of Cathy's burden.

Other props for a home school's curriculum might include part-time schooling, a tutor for a special subject, or a community education class.

The Methodology

Home schools don't have the checks and balances that formal schools have. When a public school teacher is teaching reading shabbily or distorting capitalism or ridiculing the Biblical view of creation, parents, principals, and school officials will hold him accountable.

However, home school teachers have no mandatory evaluations, no required seminars, no supervisors — their isolation makes it easier to stray in the method or content of instruction. Therefore, home educators must pursue their own development by reading, attending seminars, meeting with a skilled educator, or joining a support group. Even though we have ten years of experience in home education, though we have authored a book on the subject, though we are continually advising other home schoolers, we still find our support group invaluable. We are encouraged, rebuked, reminded, and taught by our friends who also home school. Don't try to be the "Lone Ranger" of home education.

The Children

Since most friendships begin in and are nourished by school, our kids may need assistance in overcoming their disadvantage. We have encouraged our boys to join Scouts, athletic teams, and the school band. We remind them to make arrangements a day in advance, otherwise the kids make plans with someone during the school day. We let them invite a friend to vacation with us. Home schooled kids may need help building friendships so that they don't feel like outsiders.

Conclusion

The Alternatives

Many of the benefits of home schooling can be enjoyed without teaching all of your kids from K through 12. For those without the support of a husband or a home school group, or for those unable to give up their income, there are alternatives. You may be able to delay your child's entrance into school by skipping kindergarten or home schooling for one or two years. You may be able to give one of your children a reprieve for one year. You may be able to combine part-time schooling and part-time work. You may be able to join other families and hire someone to teach a subject that you don't have the time or the skills to teach.

The Challenge

Stephen Clark believes that we seriously err when we turn children "over to schools and other social institutions for the bulk of their formation and training. New Testament childrearing practices differed drastically from this model. The parents were expected to raise the children to become mature adult Christian men and women."[22]

But training kids can be a troubling task. They are not the nice, sweet, easily moldable beings that many books on family life write about. (Whose kids are they describing? Certainly not ours.) Most kids would rather read comics than classics. They would rather watch T.V. than create a poem. They would rather play than help with housework. But don't dismiss home education simply because it is difficult. Anything worthwhile is costly.

PART TWO

VOCATIONAL TRAINING

4

THE
TRANSFORMATION
OF WORK

They had had jobs, but they had no work in the sense of a lifelong calling.[1]

A bumper sticker proclaimed: "The worst day of fishing is better than the best day of work." A group of retirees grumbled that they were "sick of working," they "hated the pressure," they had "paid their dues," and they wanted "to get out of the rat race."[2] We daydream about our weekends, vacations, retirement. The "Monday-morning-blues" is a national epidemic.

What has soiled the reputation of work? How did a gift of God become a curse? Though attitudes toward work have always fluctuated, they have eroded in Western culture since the nineteenth century when work shifted to the factory or the office, away from the home. When one boot manufacturer could produce as many boots in a year as the thirty-two thousand bootmakers of Paris, the individual craftsmen were forced to work in the factories. "Hus-bands" (*house + bonded*) were no longer bound to their homes. Though the industrial revolution benefited workers in some ways (e.g., it raised their standard of living), it diminished them in others.

The Loss of Family Life

Jane, thirteen, plays on a school volleyball team, studies piano, and talks constantly to her friends — either by phone or in person. Jane's ten-year-old brother, Eric, sings in the church choir and plays on several sports teams. He, too, relishes time with his friends trading baseball cards or riding bikes. Jane and Eric's mother, Emily, is even busier. Besides part-time work as an accountant, she serves on a church committee, volunteers at a retirement home, teaches a neighborhood Bible study — plus all of her household responsibilities. Emily's husband, Bill, owns and manages a thriving dry cleaning business that is opening two new stores in the suburbs. Bill's office is about an hour from home so he is seldom home before seven o'clock. In his free time he plays golf with his friends, serves as a deacon in his church, and visits prisoners at the local jail. When is there time for families?

Life was more simple and unified in traditional society. Kids and adults shared the same tasks, the same friends, the same leisure. But when my family wants to spend time with another family, do we choose the family of one of Nathan's friends? Or Andrew's? Or Jered's? Or Cathy's? Or mine? Someone often feels disappointed when the choice is made. Life has become more complex.

The changes in work have had a profound effect not only on the family unit but also on individual family members.

Fathers

When work exited the home, a man's day normally excluded those who knew him best — his family and his neighbors. As a result, he lost some of the pressure to be moral.

A century and a half ago, a man's success was defined by his work *and* his character. Not so today.

> Running a profitable farm or business would often have required a reputation for being a good family person and a public-spirited citizen. . . . [Now] to be a success at work means to advance up the hierarchy of [a] corporation by helping the corporation make a good profit.[3]

Most employers care only about a man's job performance — is he a good manager? Are his sales increasing? Does he complete his tasks? They aren't interested in how much time he spends with his kids or whether he is supporting his wife's growth or if he is taking time for his walk with God.

A man without accountability is vulnerable. One Christian leader whose public ministry was flourishing explained his fall into sexual sin:

> I now realize I was lacking in mutual accountability through personal relationships. We need friendships where one man regularly looks another man in the eye and asks hard questions about our moral life, our lust, our ambitions, our ego.[4]

The lack of close ties has not only affected men's character, but has also left them feeling estranged. They are working in a jungle where *true* men succeed and lesser men fail. Other men are competitors, not collaborators.

However, in traditional society a man was expected to lean on his family, his neighbors, his community. If his barn burned down, others helped rebuild it. If he became ill, friends assisted with his business. People were his life, health, and disability insurance.

Mothers

"Oh, my darling husband. How can I comfort you after your grueling day? Would you like a back rub or a cold drink?

How about a nap before dinner while our six pre-school-aged children play quietly in their rooms? Sweetie, my day was a delight. The children didn't have a single spat and helped clean the house from top to bottom. Oh, honey, it is such a joy to be your wife and the mother of your children. Really, what can I do for you?"

A realistic view of motherhood? Far from it — but not unlike the one cultivated by the industrial revolution. To counter the pressures of the workplace, the home was envisioned as "a haven in a heartless world."

> From the corroding cares of business, from the hard toil and frequent disappointments of the day, men retreat to the bosoms of their families, and there in the midst of that sweet society of wife and children and friends, receive a rich reward for their industry.[5]

Mom was confronted with "a model of the 'perfect home' — so tranquil, so cheerful, so pure, as to constitute an almost impossible standard."[6]

A mother's task in achieving this incredible standard was compounded because she lost the support of her husband and neighbors (who were at work), and her relatives (who often lived far away). And since she worked alone, she didn't know others couldn't match this fantasy either.

Guilt-ridden mothers turned to books and magazines to find help. But this distorted literature warned a woman that "if her family were not socially accepted, if her children and her husband were not healthy, . . . if she herself looked old and tired before her time, or if her babies failed to gain weight — or, worse yet, if they died — she was entirely to blame, since remedies for those conditions were easily at hand."[7]

Unfortunately, the images for moms today may be equally unachievable. One working mother complained:

[I] became afflicted with . . . the syndrome of "Everybody's Got it Together Except Me." TV commercials, popular books, and magazine articles and ads portrayed the working woman as one who juggled job, husband, home and kids, smiling all the while because "I love my work so much, it's worth it."[8]

Women not only lost support in mothering, but also lost their status as co-workers with their husbands. Thus, the economic activity of the housewife in Proverbs 31 sounds strange to us: "She considers a field and buys it; out of her earnings she plants a vineyard. . . . She sees that her trading is profitable" (Proverbs 31:16–18). The satisfaction that women gain from a career is often due to their renewed economic contribution.

Furthermore, homemakers now missed the companionship of other adults. Earlier in our marriage, my weekdays were spent arguing theology with co-workers, counseling troubled people, discussing politics with a luncheon friend. But what had Cathy done? She had changed diapers, cleaned the house, washed dishes. Her most challenging conversation was: "Does Na Na want a cracker?" By evening she hungered for communication which I was often too tired to give.

As ideals were raised and help lowered, as women were deprived of their economic role, as they were burdened with an impossible and lonely task, is it surprising that they fled to the workplace? It isn't fair to say that "a woman's place is in the home" until we confront the radical shortchanges moms have suffered in the past century.

But work outside the home has not cured most women's problems. One mother explained:

It did not occur to me that when a woman "has it all," she had to *handle it all*. To those who still insist that we can have it all I now say, Yes, indeed, all of it: an early heart attack, midnight laundry loads, and weekend catch-up headaches. There is nothing fulfilling about fatigue. Although [the feminists] . . . led us to believe that being at home with children was a consignment to boredom, they didn't remember that there are many cures for boredom, but few for the harried life of a working mother.[9]

Children

Many parents wonder if it wouldn't be easier to teach a bear to tap dance than to gain their kids' willing cooperation with housework. They often find themselves taking the easy road — they do the work rather than battle their kids' complaining and foot-dragging tactics.

However, in traditional society, children's work was a necessity. Parents could not carry the entire load. Thus, families were large, and orphanages easily placed older children. But as work left the home, children, like mothers, lost their economic value. Only bad parents depended on the labor of their children. Loved kids belonged in the "nonproductive world of lessons, games, and token money."[10] As child "experts" stated, children's work in the home was to be in the form of "some little household task," not too difficult "for their tender bodies."[11] Above all, we should "never give . . . children cause to suspect us of making use of them to save ourselves work."[12] Chores were designed to build their character, not to ease parents' burden. When children were deprived of their economic value, their self-worth languished. Now when the media trumpets the cost of raising a child — usually in the hundreds of thousands of dollars — children conclude that they are a liability rather than an asset.

Furthermore, as work left the home, kids lost models of working adults. Many believe the aimlessness of youth is a recent phenomenon; however, it is an industrial phenomenon. A book published in 1881 discussed the plight of youth:

> Young men of the present years . . . are not facing life with that resolute and definite purpose that is essential both to manhood and to external success. . . [They] hear no voice

summoning them to the appointed field, but drift into this or that, as happens.[13]

When kids are segregated from adults, they approach adulthood with a fuzzy picture of its roles and responsibilities.

Finally, as parents were drawn to the workplace, kids were left with less nurturance. Allan Bloom explains:

> Previously children at least had the unqualified dedication of one person, the woman, for whom their care was the most important thing in life. Is half the attention of two the same as the whole attention of one? Is this not a formula for neglecting children?[14]

One child, whose widowed mother worked, despaired returning to an empty house:

> Even now I remember distinctly the cold fear that enveloped me as I unlocked the front door and entered the darkened apartment. What if a burglar lurked in the dim recesses of a closet or under the bed? On those days I made a hurried examination of the premises before my body slowly relaxed.

> But even on the day when no fear stalked me, I disliked returning home to our empty apartment. No matter how sunny the weather outside, no matter how warm the air, the atmosphere of our empty home was dark and forbidding. No human voice rang out to dispel the gloom, assuring me that it was safe to enter. No mother's arms reached out to give me a welcoming hug. And if I had been wounded by a teacher or another child and came home needing attention? That need to have my self-esteem buttressed had to be ignored. Or if the day brought joy in the form of a good grade or praise? No mother was there to share in the good feelings.[15]

Children may suffer the most from our present forms of work.

Grandparents (and Extended Family)

The prosperity generated by the industrial revolution has been a two-edged sword. It has increased our financial security but lessened our need for extended family. Today's grandparents don't need their kids. The kids can make it on their own.

Though many grandparents and their children have become financially affluent, they are emotionally impoverished. Feeling needed is a key to emotional health. As my dad approached retirement age, I asked him why he was still working nearly full-time. He responded: "Because my kids need my help." He enjoys helping—and his five kids are glad he does!

Loss of Significance

The transformation of work has not only impoverished family life, but has also diminished the quality of work for many adults.

Henry Ford perfected the assembly line by dissecting the construction of a Model T into 7,882 units. Nine hundred and forty-nine of the tasks required "strong, able-bodied, and practically physically perfect men," 3,338 could be performed by men of "ordinary" strength, and the rest by women and children. He boasted that 670 of the tasks could be completed by legless men, 2,637 by one-legged men, two by armless men, 715 by one-armed men, and ten by blind men."[16] How significant can a worker feel when it doesn't take a whole body to replace him?

One summer during high school, I worked in a dairy. My primary task was to stuff cottage cheese cartons into milk cases as they hurried down a conveyor belt. The work was so boringly repetitious that I *almost* looked forward to school in the fall! One of the men I worked with had been performing similar duties for twenty years. His spirit showed it.

On the other hand, a seminary professor of mine was so enthralled with teaching that he would frequently exclaim: "I can't believe they pay me to do this!" But he was unique.

Many, many workers will spend "their working lives in a way which contains no worthy challenge, no stimulus to self-perfection, no chance of development, no element of Beauty, Truth, or Goodness."[17]

Loss of Community

Changes in work patterns have eroded our commitment to people. Recently, a local church hosted a weekend seminar. The organizer was an efficiency expert—he recruited numerous workers to greet, register, and feed the conferees. Helpers were asked to arrive at 7:30 A.M. for the 9:00 A.M. start. Signs were posted at every door to direct newcomers to the meeting room. The conference ran flawlessly. But something was missing. We helpers were never gathered to pray for the conference. We were never thanked for rising early or for giving up our Saturday—and no appreciation came the following week either. The organization of that seminar pointed to a grave defect in work today—we focus on tasks rather than people.

The industrial revolution may be largely responsible for our task orientation. Industrialized work's emphasis on efficiency, productivity, and profits has depressed the human factor. This shift from a people- to a production-minded focus did not come easily. Leo Tolstoy described this "cruel and stubborn contest" from the viewpoint of a landowner:

> On one side—his side—there was a bitter, strenuous, constant attempt to remodel everything according to [the most productive pattern], while on the other side there was the natural order of things . . . [The owner] was fighting for every penny . . . while all they were fighting for was to work calmly and pleasantly, that is, as they had been accustomed to.[18]

The early factory workers were not very productive — they stopped to chat with co-workers; they went fishing on a warm day; they stayed home to help a sick neighbor.

However, the change to a task orientation has not been universal. William McConnell recounted the story of a South American fruit peddler:

> One regular customer, who usually bought only a few pieces of fruit, once offered to buy all she had for a family party. Maria refused, although the price would have been favorable. She explained that she could buy the fruit only early in the morning; if she sold all she had before noon, she would have nothing to offer her other customers, nothing to do the rest of the day and no news to tell her family that night.[19]

How unenlightened Maria was! She could have had the rest of the day off, been assured of selling her fruit, and had time for fun. But Maria's fun was in her work — in the way it connected her with people.

Possibly, the greatest problem with work today is its failure to unite people. Many workers feel lonely because production, not people, is the goal.

Conclusion

The industrial revolution has produced many benefits — who wants to revert to raising and butchering their own meat, reading by candlelight, or traveling by foot or animal?

The concern lies with the revolution's legacy on the meaning and patterns of work. How can we find dignity and challenge in our work? How can we return to a people priority? How can family life be renewed?

There is no single solution to the problems. One foreign manufacturer of automobiles now assembles its cars with teams of employees. This policy of being involved in the whole process has inflated worker pride and morale.

However, the solution I advocate is to return work to the home. Edith Schaeffer has suggested that families develop a home business as an alternative to an economic system that is "a people-eating monster taking all the humanness out of the relationships."[20] Not everyone will establish a full-time family business. But all families can share work.

5

BRINGING WORK HOME

Millions of American children have little intimate contact with ANY adult. . . . Love cannot thrive in an ethos of work.[1]

A few years ago, I made a scary decision. Cathy and I analyzed it for several weeks. We weighed the pros and cons. We sought God's direction. Finally, I made the leap. I established an office at home. People are astonished—"How can you get anything done at home?" But why does home work seem foreign? Why was I uncertain? Our present culture is the misfit. In fact, the word *housework* was nonexistent and unnecessary before the nineteenth century because nearly all work was done around the home.

An early reviewer of this section believed that my proposals were too idealistic and would only heap guilt on already guilt-ridden parents. That is not my intent. All families can benefit from working together, even if it is not a full-time family business.

The Benefits of Home Work

All work is flawed. But some work is superior to others. The following is my pitch for family-centered work.

Fathers

In the midst of a parachurch ministry, I admitted to my boss that I was looking for a position in a church. He shocked me by asking for my immediate resignation. I was devastated! Where would we go? How could I provide for my family? Unfortunately for my anxious heart, but fortunately for my spiritual life, those concerns were not resolved quickly. Without the hindrance of busyness, I spent more time in God's word, in prayer, in evaluation. As a result, I found I had been narrowly focused on my work. At the time we had a one-year-old son and another in production. Cathy was adjusting to motherhood, and I had been insensitive to her changing needs. We also had unmet neighbors. Furthermore, while I had been feeding others, I hadn't replenished myself. The next three months became a rich (though stressful) time as I sought to respond to a variety of God-ordained tasks:

As a child of God:

Love the Lord your God with all your heart and with all your soul and with all your mind and with all your strength. (Mark 12:30)

As a husband:

Husbands, love your wives, just as Christ loved the church. (Ephesians 5:25)

As a father:

Fathers, do not exasperate your children; instead, bring them up in the training and instruction of the Lord. (Ephesians 6:4)

As a child:

If anyone does not provide for his relatives, and especially for his immediate family, he has denied the faith and is worse than an unbeliever. (1 Timothy 5:8)

As a worker:

Serve wholeheartedly, as if you were serving the Lord, not men, because you know that the Lord will reward everyone for whatever good he does. (Ephesians 6:7–8)

As a member of Christ's body:

Be devoted to one another in brotherly love. (Romans 12:10)

As a light to the world:

Let your light shine before men, that they may see your good deeds and praise your Father in heaven. (Matthew 5:16)

Home work frees men to organize their lives according to God's eternal priorities. A father who works at home can work fifteen hours one week and fifty the next, or take an afternoon off, or spend a month on the mission field. His flexibility makes it easier to serve the unpredictable needs of people — a son who cannot find a playmate for the third day in a row, a wife whose allergies make mothering seem impossible, a depressed friend who has recently been fired from his job.

Dads, working at home is good for your physical health as well. At the turn of the century, men lived nearly as long as women. Today men die almost a decade sooner. One study found that men who are self-employed live longer than those who work for someone else.[2] Apparently the pressures of the workplace contribute to an earlier death.

Mothers

The New Testament is clear—women are called to give wholeheartedly to their homes. Paul instructed older women to "train the younger women to love their husbands and children, to be self-controlled and pure, to be busy at home, to be kind, and to be subject to their husbands" (Titus 2:4–5).

But God's design for homemaking is not limited to diapers and dishes. Increase Mather's mother was typical of other seventeenth-century homemakers: "She made the decisions about hiring farmhands and domestic servants, buying and selling cattle or poultry, planting and harvesting—a role quite contrary to the submissive and subordinate role wives are usually thought to have played in seventeenth-century English society."[3] Her life was patterned after the Biblical model—"out of her earnings she plants a vineyard." Unfortunately, modern work has created a dilemma for women—they often must choose between work and family. One mother complained:

> There are a lot of [mixed-up] women in my generation. I don't know the right thing to do. I don't know how you can balance work and having children. It's not that work is so important. It's that you don't want to be confined to a family.[4]

Home work is one way to solve the dilemma. It restores women's pride in contributing to the family's economy.

Furthermore, family work also rejuvenates support for moms. My working at home allows Cathy to enjoy lunch with a friend, to run a few errands, to be recharged by a nap, to share her daily sorrows and joys with an adult. By locating my office next to the playroom, I help settle skirmishes—which are out of Mom's hearing range—before they become wars, which are not out of anyone's hearing range!

But can we expect wives who don't have their husbands' support to stay home? Consider: working mothers seldom make a large impact on the family budget; they have difficulty finding challenging work; and they still shoulder the primary burden at home. One study found that employed wives average twenty-six *hours* per week of housework while their husbands contribute a meager thirty-six *minutes* per week![5] (Don't calculate the ratio, men; it's embarrassing.) It is popular today for husbands to put on a show of assistance, but it is seldom more than theatrics. One mother concluded:

> Women with young children and an average job . . . were probably leading daily lives that were less liberated than that of their stay-at-home mothers. Today, many women working outside the (ome have less time to pursue their own interests and are no longer their own bosses as women were as housewives.[6]

Consider the liberation of one homemaker—Cathy. It is the first day of summer vacation, and Cathy is playing golf with our three sons. Throughout the summer, they will bike, picnic, swim, and fish together. She will assist the household budget by raising fresh produce, canning and freezing, and by supervising the boys' yard service. Yesterday she fixed a meal for a family with a newborn. Most days she finds time for Bible study and prayer. Could she be more fulfilled by a career?

The vigor of a stay-at-home mom is sustained by leaning on others—home school support groups, learning cooperatives, prayer and Bible study groups, an intimate friend. Someday the church may help. But at present it slumbers.

> Churches spend thousands of dollars on day-care centers, but little or nothing on services or ministries for women who choose to stay home. And if a woman who stays home does suffer economic calamity—if her husband leaves, dies, divorces her, or becomes disabled—the church helps her find a job (keeping her away from her children when they may need her the most).[7]

Children

Self-worth. "How much we gettin' paid, Dad?" my boys asked when we first began a lawn care service.

"About fifty dollars per cutting," I answered.

Their salaries had already been negotiated so they quickly added and subtracted and asked indignantly: "Well, how come we only get fifteen dollars and you get thirty-five dollars each time? We do more work than you do!"

I explained that the thirty-five dollars wasn't *my* money. It was the family's money to be used for groceries, house payments, and dental bills. I also explained that if they received all of the money, then I would have to take an additional job. I wouldn't have time to coach their soccer teams or read many books with them.

According to sociologist Viviana Zelizer, most parents rely on expressions of love to convince kids of their worth. Her view, however, is that a child depends on achievement to assess his worth.[8] Scripture has a similar view: "Each one should test his own actions. Then he can take pride in himself, without comparing himself to somebody else, for each one should carry his own load" (Galatians 6:4–5). A child's ability to shoulder responsibility, or "carry his own load," is the basis of a good self-image. As mentioned, sc(ool achievement provides kids with an appraisal of their worth, but there are few alternatives if they are not Einsteins. (This lack of options contributes to sports' dominance in youth culture — it provides another measure of worth.) When kids contribute to the family budget, when they help *significantly* with household work, when they earn money for a family vacation, or when they can point to a full woodpile, they have concrete evidence of their worth.

Vocational training. Growing and selling pumpkins to earn money for a vacation has become a family tradition. In the process, the boys have learned truths that could lead to a profession in horticulture. They have learned how to grow seedlings. They can recognize and control the insects that attack pumpkins. They know that all weeds must be pulled or their seeds will make weeding even more difficult next year.

Recently, I attended a seminar for commercial strawberry growers. One principle I *heard* was to grow the berries in previously weed-free ground. But I didn't *learn* the lesson until we planted in an area that had been infested with weeds the year before. The hours of labor, the sunburned and tired backs, and the sore knees drilled home the lesson of weed-free ground. Home work can wed the theory and practice of a profession for kids.

Social skills. Chris bounds up to the house and raps enthusiastically on the door. An elderly gentleman opens the door, and Chris begins his sales pitch:

"Hi, I'm Chris Larson. I'm selling vegetables that we grew for ourselves and . . . "

Before he can finish his speech, the man answers gruffly, "I don't want any!"—and slams the door.

Chris is crushed. Running back to the pickup with tears in his eyes, he asks, "How could anyone be so mean?"

In the midst of his hurt, his dad talks about the elderly man—is he lonely? Bitter? Ill? Chris and his dad bow their heads and pray for the man in the house.

The world is full of unlovely people. By working with my kids, I can teach them how to respond to such people. If Chris had not been with his dad, he would have probably degraded the elderly man or himself. Social skills are the most difficult skills for kids to learn—and they won't be learned without a mature guide.

A father's influence. The greatest benefit of home work to kids may be the restoration of the weighty influence of a dad. Various studies have found that the average father spends less than ten minutes a week communicating with his children.

Boys with absent fathers are more impulsive, less responsible, and more delinquent. They have difficulty making friends and are less popular with their peers. More of them drop out of school, and those who stay don't perform as well as others. And they tend to be effeminate. Similarly, girls with uninvolved fathers have more emotional and academic problems. They also relate poorly to the opposite sex.[9]

The earlier a father's absence begins, the more a child is wounded — which is troubling because most fathers are busiest when their kids are young. They are founding a business, attempting to please a new boss, working two jobs to pay for the house, the car, the furniture. The prophet Malachi pointed out that when renewal comes, God "will turn the hearts of the fathers to their children, and the hearts of the children to their fathers" (4:6). The evidence is clear — one of Satan's most poisoning works is to drive a wedge between fathers and their children.

It isn't just a child's personality that is stamped by his relationship with his dad. It also molds his view of God. Over and over in the New Testament — seventeen times in the Sermon on the Mount — God is described as our Father. I find it sobering that my model of fatherhood will contour my boys' understanding of their eternal Father.

Fathers, your kids would choose you over a new car or a membership in the country club or steak twice a week or a bedroom of their own or vacations in Florida. Scripture reminds us of our children's real need: "Fathers, do not exasperate your children; instead, bring them up in the training and instruction of the Lord" (Ephesians 6:4). Kids need more than token involvement in their lives. Sadly, many of us are committed to jobs that make fathering an infrequent vocation.

The Liabilities of Home Work

If this sounds too idyllic — it is! Family work has its problems. By the time I completed seminary, I had been a ward of schools for over twenty years. My days were regimented by class times, exam schedules, and due dates. After graduation, though, I no longer had a pedagogue. I had to decide when to study, which seminars to attend, whom to serve, what deadlines to set. That first year was laden with anxiety as I struggled with self-discipline.

Similar adjustments were necessary when I moved my office home. I was annoyed when a boy wandered into my office. I felt guilty when I took an afternoon for a family outing. The family was frustrated that I was not always available, even though I was home. I was irritated when Cathy interrupted my work to talk about a family problem.

Furthermore, a family business can be overwhelming. One study found that the self-employed worked an average of ten hours *more* per week than other workers.[10] Since the work can't be left at the office, it is tempting to work through the dinner hour or avoid vacations.

Finally, finances may be a problem. Home businesses seldom worry about how to invest their excess profits — they don't have any! When money is tight, it is difficult for parents to hide that fact from their co-working children. As a result, the kids may carry burdens that are too heavy for them. Furthermore, when money is short, kids may not be adequately compensated for their work. But Proverbs reminds us of what is most important: "Better a meal of vegetables where there is love than a fattened calf with hatred" (15:17).

Conclusion

Our family believes that the assets of home work far outweigh the liabilities. And we are able to enjoy most of these benefits through part-time, small business ventures. In the following chapter I will give suggestions on how families can inaugurate home work.

6

FAMILY WORK: GETTING YOUR HANDS DIRTY

Now the LORD God had planted a garden in the east, in Eden. . . . The LORD God took the man and put him in the Garden of Eden to work it and take care of it. (Genesis 2:8, 15)

F amily work has little support. Economist Scott Burns pointed out that annually 120 thousand graduates step into various business fields—"people devoted to the administration, management, and control of the institutions of the money economy."[1] On the other hand,

> the economy of the home attracts much less attention; a mere ten thousand degrees are awarded annually in home economics, a discipline that is still largely concerned with the quality of cake frosting and exploiting the versatility of the sewing machine. The household economy suffers from neglect.[2]

I am not naive. This book cannot do for the home economy what the hundreds of thousands of business graduates have done for the money economy. It will take much more than these few chapters to establish healthy home work.

But the need for assistance is expanding. Thomas Miller reports that there are about five million "telecommuters"—employees who perform part or all of their work at home.[3] The magazine *Family Computing* has changed its name to *Home-Office Computing* to serve these mushrooming numbers.

"What Could We Do?"

You may have heard stories about the New York executives who quit their $100,000 per year jobs, sell their homes and belongings, and head for the Alaskan wilderness to build a log cabin and live off the land. Though some of us may make such radical changes, the majority of us weaker-willed souls look for safer options.

I have a prejudice—I believe that some of the best family businesses are those that depend on the land. I say this, first, because of the value God places on His creation. The ark included animals. The curses and blessings on Israel focused on its relationship to its "soil, its vineyards, its produce, its animals"[4] (see Deuteronomy 28). When Jesus returns, creation "will be liberated from its bondage to decay and brought into the glorious freedom of the children of God" (Romans 8:21).

Furthermore, I am enthused about working close to creation because:

> The heavens declare the glory of God;
> the skies proclaim the work of his hands.
> Day after day they pour forth speech;
> night after night they display knowledge.
> (Psalms 19:1–2)

While working on the land, I am continually confronted with the God who made the land—a startling sunset, the wonders of plants from seeds, a dramatic thunderstorm, the marvels of honey bees.

Working the land is also beneficial because physical exercise enhances our emotional lives. After spending a couple hours in the garden, I find that I am renewed and ready to write again.

Finally, those who work with God's creation gain the satisfaction of nurturing the entire process—unlike most factory workers. Our family orders seeds for our garden in January. The seedlings sprout under our grow-lights while the outside world slumbers. We plant hardy seedlings in a greenhouse surrounded by patches of snow. We begin harvesting lettuce and spinach in April, followed by asparagus, peas, strawberries, broccoli, cauliflower, raspberries, zucchini, beans, cucumbers, onions, potatoes, peppers, tomatoes, corn, cantaloupe, squash, and pumpkins.

Working with God's creation, then, could involve a multitude of choices—fruit orchards, ranches, egg farms, fish farms, raising flowers or vegetables, breeding dogs or horses, a tree nursery, beekeeping. It will, of course, take time to determine where your interests and local needs intersect.

A vision, though, of families working together cannot be confined to those willing to wear coveralls and John Deere caps. As David Shi observed: "Proponents of the simple life have frequently been overly nostalgic about the quality of life in olden days [and] narrowly anti-urban in outlook."[5] Many of us who are anxious about giving up the convenience of city life can still find home work in the city. The possibilities include: a lawn care service, paper routes, a flower shop, an income tax service, a catering service, book binding, a cleaning service, refinishing and selling antiques, auto repair, writing children's books, a handyman service, an amusement center, a pet kennel, managing rental properties, an engine repair shop, a typing service, a bakery, exercise classes, a book store, a bicycle repair shop, or a health food store. It may be possible to keep your present job but work at home. Some firms have found that sending workers home saves office space and expenses, as well as increasing productivity by as much as twenty-five percent.

Even without a full-time home business, families can still work together. Our family balances a variety of work. As stated, I write at home. But since writers earn about as much as kids running a lemonade stand, I am also teaching part-time at a local college. As a family, we have two small businesses—a lawn service and door-to-door sales of garden produce. We also labor together in the ongoing tasks of maintaining a house, a yard, and a car, and in special tasks like cleaning the church, helping a friend paint his house, or shoveling the walks for an elderly neighbor. Some families have invested time in special work projects (e.g., building a house or helping on a missions project) by taking a sabbatical or extra vacation time from their jobs. A full-time family business is the ideal, but creative alternatives are still worthwhile.

"How Can We Pull It Off?"

The first commodity required to begin family work is time, which is about as rare as a windless day on the prairie. Time can be redeemed from your present work. Many businesses allow job sharing (two employees dividing one job) or flextime (working other than an eight to five schedule). Still other companies pay employees by the job rather than the clock. Finally, mom could resign from her job (if she is working) and invest time in a family business.

Not only do you need time, but you need to take your time. A few years ago, we planted a small apple orchard at my parents' farm. Everything went well until the middle of the summer, which is often hot and *dry* in South Dakota. We discovered that hauling water to thirsty trees was a major project. We worked hard but eventually lost over half of the trees.

We learned an important lesson—begin small. Otherwise, your education may be expensive! Take your time. Test your interests and skills. Determine if there are markets for your product or service. See if it will be financially rewarding.

"How Can We Afford It?"

Materialism is not only a modern disease. Solomon warned of its dangers: "Do not wear yourself out to get rich; have the wisdom to show restraint" (Proverbs 23:4). Socrates complained that "many people will not be satisfied with the simpler way of life. They will be for adding sofas, and tables, and other furniture; also dainties, and perfumes, and incense, and courtesans and cakes."[6] Sound familiar?

You may wonder whether you can afford to have mom quit her job. But consider the impact that Cathy has on our budget by being our barber. It was costing us men about twenty-five dollars a month to get our hair cut. So our yearly savings is three hundred dollars, right? Wrong! Other factors must be added to the equation. The twenty-five dollars we were spending was what remained after we paid Social Security, income tax, and tithes. Our haircuts also included parking and auto expenses. In addition, if Cathy had worked we would have had additional expenses for day-care and an expanded wardrobe. Thus, by this one job of barbering, we have to earn about five hundred to six hundred dollars *less* per year. But a mom can do far more than cut hair. She can sew and mend clothes, bake bread, and raise fruits and vegetables. She can cook meals from scratch rather than depend on restaurants or prepared foods. She has time to be a discriminating shopper. And she will also have time to invest in a family business.

It is difficult to live simply in a world of extravagance. As Eliot Daley stated, "It sure is hard to live by what you believe, when everything around you says to live by what you see."[7] Family businesses seldom offer the material rewards that standard jobs do. You may be forced to drive a dented, rusting VW rather than a BMW, to vacation in a tent rather than in a condo on the Gulf of Mexico, to recover your old sofa rather than replace it. Your fine dining may consist of a Big Mac and fries rather than a seven-course French dinner.

Those willing to accept a lower standard of livng have learned that "a man's life does not consist in the abundance of his possessions" (Luke 12:15). They have been enriched by other rewards:

> Jeff, my first-grader, remains tucked cosily in bed until eight while his day-care counterparts are hurried through break-fast, dressed and dropped off with a quick kiss. Working at home, I'm also able to etch memories for him of fresh ba-nana bread and the sound of the crackling fire he loves coming home to on gray Seattle days.[8]

"Go for It!"

Throughout my twenties and early thirties I had a kalei-doscope of vocational dreams. The shapes and colors of those dreams shifted as Light was shed in my life. I remember many sleepless nights when I became dazzled by the sights — serving God on a college campus, preaching the gospel to unreached peoples, shepherding a body of believers, teaching at a Chris-tian college, teaching at a secular college, raising fruits and vegetables, communicating God's truth through writing, working in my dad's cheese business, counseling families, de-veloping a retreat ministry for burned out pastors — the list goes on. But as I reached my mid-thirties, I realized that I had to choose one or two of those visions and say no to the others. God has gifted each of us differently. "He appointed some to be . . . others to be . . ." We must discern what those gifts are and how God can use them. As I concluded my early adult years, I felt God nudging me toward writing. It fit my gifts and desires. It fit the style of family life that we wanted. But it was not a safe choice. At that point, I was an unpub-lished author and knew it would be at least several years before I could earn much money. Though it was not an easy decision, one thought sealed it—I knew that when I reached my sixties, failure would be less troublesome than regret, "What if I had only . . ."

The leap can be difficult, even after prayer and cautious planning. Fear can paralyze you. "What if we have misjudged the market?" "What if we can't pay our bills?" "What if we can't provide our kids with a college education?" "What if . . . what if . . ." Joshua faced even greater "what-ifs" when he replaced Moses and led a suspect people against the powerful Canaanites. But God knew Joshua's need:

> Be strong and courageous, for you must go with this people into the land that the LORD swore to their forefathers to give them. . . . The LORD himself goes before you and will be with you; he will never leave you nor forsake you. Do not be afraid; do not be discouraged. (Deuteronomy 31:7–8)

Are you afraid to take the risk? The antidote for fear is to remind yourself repeatedly—as God did with Joshua—that God "will never leave you nor forsake you."

Conclusion

There is a crisis in work. We know pastors with young families who give overwhelming priority to formal ministry. We know fathers who pray for work to slow down, but can't when it does. We know stay-at-home moms who feel guilty when asked, "And what do you do?" We know dads who don't know the names of their children's closest friends. We know mothers who work full time but agonize over their choice:

> I'm torn. I'm two people. . . . The worst of it is that I feel like I'm doing a lousy job both at home and in my [job]. . . . Already I have regrets about not spending enough time with [my children], and I know that once

they are grown and gone I'll live with the guilt and regret for the rest of my life.[9]

Furthermore, the crisis has cooled connections within families:

When we [fathers] are home, we are either dressing, eating, and rushing out the door or dashing in tired, needing to relax and unwind. The structure of [a father's] day is a built-in barrier to intimacy between father and child. Confronted by it, we do what human beings do so well: adapt. Children stifle their feelings for their fathers; fathers numb themselves to their capacity for nurturance; and both lose themselves in other things.[10]

Something radical is needed. We can't continue to assume that standard jobs are a must, that the forty-hour work week with two weeks of vacation is the Biblical model, that children can be nurtured on fifteen minutes of "quality" time each day. Open yourself to God's leading — "Am I where You want me vocationally, Lord? Are there better alternatives?"

The solution I offer — bringing work home — is certainly not the only solution to the dilemma of families. But we need to think creatively about how to meet the needs of the troubled, modern family.

7

CHILDREN AND WORK

Childhood is the time when children establish either a firm sense of industry — that they can do a job and do it well — or an abiding sense of inferiority, a sense that whatever they undertake will end badly.

David Elkind

Character is a by-product: it is produced in the great manufacture of daily duty.

Woodrow Wilson

Johnny, would you please empty the waste baskets?"

"Oh, Mom, how come I always have to empty them? Why can't Joe do it once in a while?"

"Okay. I'll let him do that. You can mow the lawn."

"Mow the lawn? You've got to be kidding. It's 140 degrees outside. I'll have a heat stroke."

"Jonathan, if you don't get moving and do one of those jobs, you're not going to get your allowance."

"That's okay. I've got enough money anyway."

"Listen, Jonathan Ray Johnston. I am not giving you a choice! You get busy and get that work done."

If family work is going to be effective our children must be cooperative. When Paul addressed workers he exhorted them to work "with sincerity of *heart*"; to do "the will of God from [the] *heart*" (Ephesians 6:5–7, emphasis added); to work "*wholeheartedly*" (see Colossians 3:22–23). Home work is a joke if our kids don't have their hearts in it.

Transmitting God's View of Work

Our children will be willing workers if they adopt God's perspective on work. That perspective involves four concepts.

Work Is a Gift from God

Americans aren't enthused about their work — at least that is the perception of children. Primary school children were asked if adults liked work. The study found that the older the child, the more negatively he rated adult attitudes toward work. Whereas nearly half of the first graders thought adults enjoyed their work, only seventeen percent of the fifth graders believed they did.[1]

But work is a vital part of God's design for life. "The LORD God took the man and put him in the Garden of Eden to work it and take care of it" (Genesis 2:15). As pastor John Stott has explained, we live in a world

> in which we depend on God but also (we say it reverently) He depends on us. . . . He did not create the planet earth to be productive on its own; human beings had to subdue and develop it. He did not plant a garden whose flowers would blossom and fruit ripen on their own; He appointed a gardener to cultivate the soil.[2]

What a high calling! The God of the universe and I are partners. Whether in agriculture or human services or the arts, I can contribute to God's work.

Again, though, this is not the view of work most of us parents communicate to our kids. During a recent mowing season, I became increasingly frustrated. Our lawn mower was carrying on an affair with its repairman, I was busy with a new part-time job, and a warm spring was causing the grass to grow faster than Jack's beanstalk! I didn't realize how bad my attitude was until I saw it mirrored in my boys. In their whining—"Oh, Dad, do we have to mow again? It seems like we just did it."—and their verbal abuse of the mower—"You dumb mower! Why won't you start?"—I saw my reflection. I should have considered it a privilege to work with my boys and earn a good wage for our labor.

Moms, what attitudes do you portray toward meal preparation? Dads, do your wives have to cajole you into doing household repairs? What attitudes do you bring home about your job—complaints? anger? thankfulness? If work is something we grudgingly perform, our children will never view work as a gift from their heavenly Father.

Work Serves God

God is our employer: "Whatever you do, work at it with all your heart, as working for the Lord, not for men, since you know that you will receive an inheritance from the Lord as a reward" (Colossians 3:23–24).

After serving as the pastor of a small church for several years, I found that some in the congregation questioned my motives. I was shocked and angered. How could I be so misjudged? I labored to answer their concerns but was unsuccessful. As a result, the church dissolved. Cathy and I became depressed. Why bother? Why risk rejection again? Only one thought sustained us—we knew our heavenly Father "sees in secret" and will reward righteousness. To work wholeheartedly, our children must be able to look beyond frail, human praise to the sturdy, heavenly praise. God will reward them for not grumbling over the unjust treatment of a boss, for serving an ungracious fellow worker, or for working conscientiously without recognition.

Work Serves People

God also designed work to serve others. Stott reminds us that we depend on each other not only for:

> the basic needs of physical life (food, clothing, shelter, warmth, safety, and health care) but also everything which makes up the richness of human life (education and recreation, sport, travel and culture, music, literature, and the arts), not to mention spiritual nurturing. So whatever our job—in one of the professions (education, medicine, the law, the social services, architecture or construction), in national or local politics or the civil service, in industry, commerce, farming or the media, . . . or in the home, we need to see it as being cooperation with God, in serving the needs of human beings.[3]

Paul reflected this priority of service when he commanded thieves to work so that they would "have something to share with those in need" (Ephesians 4:28).

Serving employers. As I teach my boys about work, I want to help them focus on others. It begins with serving their employers. Paul commanded workers to please their masters "not only when their eye is on you and to win their favor, but with sincerity of heart and reverence for the Lord" (Colossians 3:22). When mowing lawns, we don't want to habitually arrive a day or two late, letting the lawn become shaggy. Furthermore, we let our yard owners periodically evaluate our work to determine if it meets their standards.

Serving employees. The Pharisees were aghast—Jesus' disciples violated the Sabbath by picking grain. But Jesus explained: "The Sabbath was made for man, not man for the

Sabbath" (Mark 2:27). Jesus could have said the same thing about work—"Work was made for man, not man for work."—because work also can dominate rather than serve. So that our "workers" (i.e., our kids) are not abused in the home economy, we must understand their needs.

One of those needs is *responsibility*. "But, Dad, how come I have to stay home to do the laundry? All the other kids are at the swimming pool." We may feel like ogres when we require our kids to help with household work. But is "it good for a child to remain a privileged guest who is thanked and praised for 'helping out,' rather than a collaborator who at a certain age is expected to assume his or her fair share of household duties?"[4] God's perspective is that "it is good for a man to bear the yoke while he is young" (Lamentations 3:27). Daily chores develop diligence, perseverance, and productivity in our kids.

The responsible child completes a task. Recently, Cathy became exasperated with the boys' messes around the house—combs and brushes in the bathroom, food containers on kitchen counters, dishes at the dinner table, dirty clothes in their bedrooms. Though not any one mess was overwhelming, Cathy found herself either nagging them or doing the jobs herself. So we announced a new policy: if a child has to be reminded to clean up a mess, they will have to complete that chore plus another one. After a few days the messes "magically" became fewer.

But we must be careful not to burden kids with overwhelming tasks. When our boys first made their beds, it often looked like their toys were trapped under the covers—and sometimes they were! Frequently, Cathy would later smooth out the lumps. One day when she was trying to persuade Andrew (who was five at the time) to make his bed, he dejectedly complained: "But Mom, I can't do it as good as you can." He had reasoned that Mom wasn't satisfied with his work, so why try? Kids will dump lawn clippings on newly sprouted lettuce, use half a bottle of Windex to wash the

windows, substitute baking soda for baking powder in the
pancakes, spill a quart of oil on a clean garage floor. Certainly
they can be reminded to be careful or taught better tech-
niques. But initially, we may have to accept lower standards.

Another need that our kids have is *fellowship*. All too frequently when I share work with my boys, I am preoccupied
with completing the task—and thus, am blinded to their
needs. But taking a twenty minute break from mowing to
drink a milk shake and talk with them is equally important. I
want them to learn that life is not to be filled with frantic
activity—"In repentance and rest is your salvation, in quietness and trust is your strength" (Isaiah 30:15). We need unhurried time for friendships, prayer, thought.

A third need is *individuality*. Andrew prefers his work to
precede leisure. (It is the same trait that causes him to pick
his bacon strips out of his sandwich so that he can savor the
crunchy strips at the end of the meal.) Thus, he is a steady
worker from beginning to end. On the other hand, Nathan
likes to spread out his misery. His preference is
work/play/work/play. The solution is not to demand confor-
mity. We give them a time frame in which the work must be
done and let them manage their own work. If they act irre-
sponsibly, then we set different restrictions (e.g., no play until
work is done).

Our children also need a *challenge*. Before Jesus' return to
heaven, He issued a challenge that has captivated Christians
for centuries: "All authority in heaven and on earth has been
given to me. Therefore go and make disciples of all nations,
baptizing them in the name of the Father and of the Son and
of the Holy Spirit, and teaching them to obey everything I
have commanded you" (Matthew 28:18–20).

Challenge is important for kids' work, too. If their jobs are
limited to emptying wastebaskets and clearing off the table,
they will be bored. On the other hand, if they can paint a
room, build a deck, repair a car, clean the gutters, transplant
a bush, shampoo the carpets, shop for groceries, sew their

clothes, or cook a meal, they will be more cooperative. Furthermore, by performing the meaty jobs in a household, they
sense they are truly needed.

Finally they need *evaluation*. Like the Seven Dwarfs, Andrew usually whistles while he works. But on occasion, he can
be grumpier than an overworked waitress. I find it much easier
to rebuke a grumbling child — "Andrew, if you don't straighten
up I'm going to give you more work to do!" — than praise a
cheerful one — "Andrew, God sure is pleased that you enjoy
your work." Evaluation involves correction *and* encouragement.

Working Together. Family work is just that — it is a family
working *together*. When picking up the basement seems overwhelming to an exhausted child, we can help. When a boy
complains about mowing the lawn, we can remind him that
life is filled with unwanted, but necessary, tasks. When weeding on a hot day seems meaningless, we can remind him of
the fishing vacation that the garden will fund. If we want to
implant God's truth about work in our kids, we must work
with them.

Vocational Training Outside the Home

Though the home can provide the foundation for a vocation, it is completed by other experiences. But even in these
complimentary experiences, the home plays a key role.

Schooling

When we think of vocational training, we think of
schools first. But schools are often not the place to begin.
This is true, first, because schools deal with the theory rather
than the practice of a profession. How many people spent
years and thousands of dollars preparing to be teachers, law-
yers, engineers, chemists, businessmen, but when they settled
into a job, found it didn't fit their gifts or interests? Prior experience could have avoided an extravagant waste of time

and money. Furthermore, schools cannot accurately predict job markets. Cathy majored in math with thoughts of teaching. But her counselor advised that a teaching certificate wouldn't be necessary because of the high demand for math instructors. Two years after graduation, a large number of laid-off engineers rushed to teaching, making it impossible for Cathy to find a job.

Finally, the vocational advice of schools may be suspect because most departmental cuts or increases are made on the basis of student enrollment, not the availability of jobs in that field. Thus, some professors push students toward their courses to secure their jobs. Competition for students became so intense at one school that professors tacked up posters to advertise their courses.

Teen Employment

The statistics of teenagers who work are impressive. By the time students graduate from high school, over eighty percent have held a job. On the surface this appears to be encouraging—kids being initiated into the "real world." But there are serious problems with the pattern of teenage work, as Ellen Greenberger and Laurence Steinberg cautioned in their timely book, *When Teenagers Work.*[5]

First, teenage work squeezes out important experiences for kids. Sixty-three percent of high school seniors work an average of twenty-one hours per week during the school year.[6] When this is added to the hours spent in school (thirty plus), it is easy to see that their time is pinched for doing homework, working on a school newspaper, reading, building a friendship, or participating in band, sports, and church activities.

Secondly, most teenage work is unrelated to later adult work—nearly half of the teens are employed as food service workers and store clerks. In traditional society, a child eased into adult life by apprenticing in the work that he would be doing as an adult. But a job at Wendy's seldom leads to a career as a fast food manager.

A third weakness of teenage work is it seldom brings kids into greater contact with adults. Normally teens work with peers and have twenty-one-year-old "adult" managers. When teens work with elders, they are as apt to be training them (e.g., demonstrating the proper technique of wrapping a taco) as the other way around. Though children's work in earlier America had other problems, it had:

> an important advantage over its counterpart today: turn-of-the-century factories, farms, shops, and mills put young people in touch with adult members of the community, adults from whom they learned about work, about the expectations of the community with respect to being an adult, about their strengths and foibles.[7]

Even when teens work with an adult, it is seldom with a family friend or acquaintance — as it was in traditional society. Instead, they usually work for strangers who seldom "perceive themselves as having a legitimate stake in the young person's development."[8]

Fourth, Greenberger and Steinberg found that contrary to popular thought, teen work did not keep kids out of trouble. In fact, it increased delinquency and drug use among some workers.

Finally, and most surprisingly, the authors found that teenage employment did not teach responsibility in the use of money because the bulk of teens' earnings are spent with few guidelines or restrictions. Few help with family expenses. Few save any money. Few tithe. As a result, these kids experience "premature affluence." Earning a couple hundred dollars a month may not seem like a lot, but when it can be spent on any whim or fad, it may be more spending money than many adults have. Thus, "it is debatable whether being responsible for how one uses one's money is the same thing as learning to use money responsibly."[9]

The problems with your teenager working are not insurmountable. But he will need—though he may not appreciate!—your involvement. When we enforced a savings program for our eldest, he barked, "Well, I didn't ask for an agent!"

It is much easier to let your kids spend their money freely than to "teach them that they can survive without the latest in headphones, or the newest style of cashmere sweater, or front-row seats to every concert in town."[10] Don't opt for the broad road. Besides, if you explain your concerns, most kids will be willing to have guidelines set for their work—a limit on their hours, the use of their money, the type of work.

Volunteer Work

The variety and substance of teen work is sparse. But in order to find a fit in the adult world of work, teens need a variety of experiences in which they will "encounter difficulty, frustration, challenge, excitement, questioning, and satisfaction."[11] During my final year of seminary, one professor advised us to do something different every year for the next ten years. He reasoned that our most effective ministry wouldn't come until later, and the variety would help us determine where we could serve most effectively. Though I didn't intentionally follow his advice, during the decade after graduation I gained experience as a pastor, an evangelist, a gardener, a coach, a professor, a church planter, a personnel director, a writer, and a counselor. As a result of this broad education, I know God's direction for my life.

When children are young, they use their parents' clothes in their play; they are practicing being moms and dads. Volunteer work can be similar. It allows children to try on a variety of vocational hats.

Rich opportunities are open to those who are willing to work without pay. A local Christian college wanted me to teach part-time but had no money in their budget. I agreed to teach without pay. Teens willing to work *gratis* can find positions in veterinary clinics, hospitals, libraries, retirement homes, auto repair shops, law offices, day-care centers, political organizations, and mental institutions.

However, children need parental assistance for volunteerism to work. First of all, they need help interpreting their tasks. A study of sixth-grade children who tutored mentally handicapped children found that when their work was followed by a class discussion, the students developed positive attitudes toward the retarded children.[12] Questions for such an exercise might include:

- "What did you find most surprising / most difficult / most discouraging / most encouraging about your work?"

- "What is the greatest need that these children have?"

- "Why would God allow innocent children to be born with such great deficiencies?"

- "How do you respond to people who say we should abort handicapped children?"

But the kids who didn't analyze the task developed negative attitudes. One educator summarized: "You do not learn by doing. You learn by thinking / acting / thinking / acting."[13]

Secondly, our volunteer workers need financial aid — money for the collection plate, a new blouse, a video game. We don't have to support their every whim, but we can't expect them to be penniless and remain positive toward volunteer work.

Finally, our kids need spiritual insight to fill out their volunteer work. When our eldest began working at a retirement home, he and I discussed Jesus' words in Mark 10:43: "Whoever wants to become great among you must be your ser-

vant." I explained that there are different kinds of greatness — athletic greatness, financial greatness, political greatness. But spiritual greatness comes from serving. He and I
prayed that God would use him to serve the needs of the
elderly residents.

Your job may be the best place to expose your kids to
challenging work. When one father brought his kids to his
business meetings, "tongues wagged over this strange practice." Though awkward at times, he included his kids in the
conversations: "I would explain what we were talking about,
taking pains to keep it simple and free of jargon. And quite
by accident, I found this helped me shape a controversial
issue in its most basic terms."[14]

Eventually, this businessman's kids fit in: "It was at one of
these dinners, in fact, that my son, Joshua, then fifteen, came
of age. A banker leaned over to him and asked, 'What's your
father's view on this issue?' And Joshua told him. He understood the problem, how I felt about it, and he responded as
an adult."[15] If your job allows it, both you and your children
can benefit from participating in your work.

Vocations and Vocational Ministry

The New Testament says little about vocational work.
Words like *work* and *labor* describe our task in living and pro-
claiming God's truth — "Always give yourselves fully to the
work of the Lord, because you know that your *labor* in the
Lord is not in vain" (1 Corinthians 15:58, emphasis added).

But this teaching is a call to ministry, not vocational ministry. During the years I was involved in a campus ministry, I
frequently heard statistics about the number of students from
various campuses who chose to go into "full-time Christian
service." These statistics were spoken in reverent terms — one
didn't want to sound proud! — and were used as a sign of the
vitality of a particular ministry. But how do we justify such
talk? The perspective of the New Testament is different:

"*Whatever you do*, work at it with all your heart, as working for the Lord, not for men, since you know that you will receive an inheritance from the Lord as a reward" (Colossians 3:23–24, emphasis added). I know several men who translated an enthusiasm for the faith into a call to vocational ministry. But later, sometimes much later, they suffered anguish, self-doubt, and deep feelings of guilt when they concluded they could serve God better in a different profession.

Conclusion

Educator John Holt believed the best way to prepare for a vocation is by taking the most direct route:

If you want someday to build boats, go where people are building boats, find out as much as you can. When you've learned all they know, or will tell you, move on. Before long, even in the highly technical field of yacht design, you may find you know as much as anyone.[16]

Preparation for a profession may include schooling:

If you find out that there are many things you want or need to know that the people working won't tell you, but that you can find out most easily in school, then go for that reason. [Or] if none of the people doing your chosen work will even let you in the door without some piece of school paper, you may have to pay time and money to some school to get it.[17]

But often school isn't a necessity: "There may be quicker, cheaper, and more interesting ways." As our children get older, we must help them think creatively about how to prepare for a vocation.

PART THREE

SOCIAL
TRAINING

8

SOCIALIZATION: THE LOSS OF COMMUNITY

We have a surprisingly uncritical arrogance towards the past. "Tradition" has become a bad word. We claim to know more than our ancestors, and in that way we may be correct. That does not necessarily mean that we know better.[1]

Your Sunday School class is beginning. Your leader asks for announcements. There is one about a potluck dinner, another about a retreat. Then he asks if there are any prayer requests. Joe, visibly shaking, stammers: "Karen and I are having serious problems. I almost walked out last night and we need your prayers." The room fills with an awkward silence. Everyone is stunned. Normally, prayer requests are safer—Aunt Mabel's broken toe, a child's case of the flu, a husband's need for work.

Why does such a confession sound strange? What is strange is our attempt to face life on our own. Paul told the church at Corinth: "The eye cannot say to the hand, 'I don't need you!' And the head cannot say to the feet, 'I don't need you!' " (1 Corinthians 12:21). We are severely handicapped if we don't depend on others.

Cultural changes, however, have made a difficult task — learning how to lean on others — nearly impossible. Most of us are trying to solve the enigma of life alone.

Segregation

I chuckle as I remember the stages of boy/girl relationships. They went something like this:

- First grade: girls? Yuk!

- Second grade: stuffing grasshoppers down girls' backs

- Third grade: chasing girls on the playground

- Fourth grade: writing notes to boys about girls

- Fifth grade: writing notes to girls

- Sixth grade: talking to girls

- Seventh grade: attending socials

- Eighth grade: first dates; embarrassed by family's interest

- Ninth grade: going steady/breaking up

- Tenth grade: long phone calls; letters when apart

- Eleventh grade: enjoying female companionship as much or more than male companionship

- Twelfth grade: how intimate should we become?

- Freshman: should we marry? welcome family's interest

- Sophomore: engagement

- Junior: marriage

And my learning continues—I will never wholly know even my wife. A bride of nearly forty years declared:

> You are still new, my love. I do not know you,
> Stranger beside me in the dark of bed,
> Dreaming the dreams I cannot ever enter,
> Eyes closed in that unknown, familiar head.
> Who are you . . . ?[2]

But who will steer kids through the labyrinth of love? Who will inform them that disputes can be beneficial? that one person can't meet all of their needs? that misunderstandings are unavoidable? Because of the increasing segregation of adults from children—in school, in leisure, even in church—few guides are available. As mentioned, a study of thirty-six hundred rural teens found that kids infrequently turn to adults when they encounter a problem. Parents, teachers, guidance counselors, clergy, and professional counselors were all rated in the lower half of fifty-four coping options. With adults unavailable, who do teens turn to? Music, friends, drugs, shopping, and video games. No wonder one-third of these kids reported being depressed![3]

Furthermore, when retirement homes hide the elderly, when the workplace removes adults during the day, when day-care centers conceal the very young, when hospitals house the sick and dying—children don't learn how to relate to life's diversity of people. They won't learn about the care of babies by reading a book or the needs of the elderly by singing Christmas carols at a retirement home.

But children aren't the only ones who suffer from the disjointing of the generations, as the testimony of a grandfather living in a nursing home reveals:

> My grandchildren come and see me here a couple of times
> a year. I don't even feel that I miss them. I kind of put it
> out of my mind, I guess. If I think about it I get angry . . .
> or maybe it hurts. Yeah, I guess that's it. I can't give what

I've got. I don't have the opportunity to pass it on, the funny stories.[4]

Mobility

Only one of my closest friends of the past fifteen years still lives in the same city that I do. When one of these friends recently moved, I became depressed. *Why go through the agony of building a deep friendship when it probably won't last?* Our mobility obstructs intimacy.

Mary Ann Kuharski wondered about the effect of a move by a close friend:

[Henry] uprooted his wife and children from Minnesota, friends, and familiarity for one reason: the promise of more money (read comfort level) in Oklahoma. So it was good-bye home town. Goodbye friends, neighbors, and family ties. And hello Oklahoma, and hello money. Only Henry will be able to measure if the profit is worth the loss.[5]

Jobs, more than family, church, and friends, determine where we live. When we look for work, we don't ask, "Who will look after Mom and Dad in their declining years?" We seldom think about friendships. The opportunities for Christian growth and service don't carry much weight.

A nine-year-old girl complained that she didn't like her new house: "It doesn't have memories." But if she achieves the national average she will have to establish new memories fourteen times during her lifetime![6] No wonder deep bonds are the exception rather than the rule.

Independence

"Let me do it myself!" could be our national motto.

We believe in the dignity, indeed the sacredness, of the individual. Anything that would violate our right to think for ourselves, judge for ourselves, make our own decisions, live our lives as we see fit, is not only morally wrong, it is sacrilegious.[7]

Though Americans have always valued independence, it was formerly tempered by a commitment to the community. Thus, men gave their time "serving year after year as surveyors of highways, as fence-viewers, and wardens. These tasks entailed many hours of labor — constructing town buildings, roads, fences, dams, and mills."[8]

Today, however, parents are more concerned with preparing kids for independence than teaching them social responsibility. During the 1890s, one study found that mothers believed that "strict obedience" and "loyalty" were the paramount traits to instill into children. But by the 1920s, "independence" was equally valued.[9]

What fed this emphasis on independence? The theories of Sigmund Freud had an enormous impact. We came to believe that if children "did not separate themselves effectively from their parents, they would experience disturbed relationships [in marriage] and also have trouble bringing up healthy children."[10]

Unfortunately, many Christians have been influenced more by Freud than the Bible on this issue. They assume that total separation from parents is a must. One Christian advised that "parenting is only a temporary job description"[11]and that we are to release our kids so that they "become people who don't need us anymore"[12] and that we must unravel "the ties that bind us."[13] As we will see in the next chapter, God never intended such a radical independence.

Many Americans are desperately lonely. When Northwestern Bell introduced a GABLINE — "the electronic equivalent of sitting on the front porch and talking with passing strangers" — customers responded overwhelmingly.[14] In one major city, twelve to twenty-seven thousand people each week pay a by-the-minute fee to be connected with nine other strangers to talk about whatever is on their minds. Our pursuit of independence has a price: the "freedom to be left alone is a freedom that implies being alone."[15]

Isolation

There are other changes which have cooled relationships in our culture.

Transportation

When Cathy was sent to the corner grocery store by her mother, she skipped home with a piece of licorice donated by the kindly owner. But when I visit the grocer with my boys, we know no one. My boys don't have a friend who will tell them a joke or give them a piece of candy or listen to their newest riddle.

What brought about the change? It was primarily due to advancements in transportation. Before buses, subways, and autos, merchants had to be within walking distance of their customers. Thus, "a neighborhood community was a walking community: of passers-by, of casual street corner encounters, of sidewalk greetings and doorway conversations."[16] Working men often socialized at cafes before and after work. Women's shopping was a social as well as a functional affair.

Communication Systems

Many communities have been held together by their newspapers. This vanishing breed of paper has had an important function:

> When the girl at the glove-counter marries the boy in the wholesale house, the news of their wedding is good for a forty-line wedding notice, and the forty lines in the country paper gives them self-respect. When in due course we know that their baby is a twelve-pounder named Grover or Theodore or Woodrow, we have that neighborly feeling

that breeds real democracy. When we read of death in that home we can mourn with them that mourn.[17]

But now they have been replaced, in part, by the *USA Today* with its five-line summary of what is happening in an entire state. It isn't likely many wedding or birth announcements will make that news!

On the surface, the telephone appears to enhance friendships. Though it increased the frequency of communication, it decreased the depth of interactions. If I spent thirty minutes traveling to a friend's house, I would not leave after a two-minute conversation. But if someone chats on the phone for more than five or six minutes, we become as impatient as a child waiting to open his Christmas presents.

Furthermore, changes in mail delivery increased our isolation. When we moved to Tampa, Florida, and before we found an apartment, we had to collect our mail at the post office. One day while standing in line with our gregarious one-year-old, Nathan, he greeted the man behind us with a sunny "Hi!" The dour-faced man kept staring straight ahead and said nothing. Undaunted, Nathan grinned again and said, "Hi!" Unbelievably, the man continued his blank stare, unwilling to acknowledge the greeting. But Nathan persisted: "Hi!" Finally, this hardened man looked down at Nathan, smiled, and said, "Hi, little fella." Now push this scene back one hundred years, prior to the advent of home delivery . . . we would have run into this gentleman frequently on our daily trek to the post office. As we stood in line, we would have learned one another's names and, probably, the turmoil that made it nearly impossible to respond to a toddler's joyous greeting. Rural Free Delivery? No. It has been very costly.

Community Celebrations

I have fond childhood memories of Independence Day—firecrackers, races at the swimming pool, a picnic with relatives, and a fireworks display at the golf course. The burst of colors in the sky was a metaphor of the swelling emotions inside of me.

But public celebrations — national and religious holidays, election day, militia muster day — have faded. We seldom participate in anything like the Lincoln-Douglas debates:

> All of the debates were conducted amid a carnival-like atmosphere. Bands played (although not during the debates), hawkers sold their wares, children romped, liquor was available. These were important social events as well as rhetorical performances.[18]

The loss of community events is one more reason why we feel alienated from others. (And is also one reason why sports have become dominant in our culture — they are among the few activities that still unite communities.)

Leisure

Finally, changes in leisure have stifled relationships. In traditional society, leisure included more interaction between people. It involved playing instruments, singing songs, reading books, relaxing on the front porch. One woman described her grandparents' porch:

> Many of the neighborhood children would play on her porch. . . . Her porch was a kind of day-care center for the neighborhood. While I was there my grandparents would sit on the porch and chat or visit with the neighbors, or just sit quietly watching the people coming and going. After dinner, most of the people on the street would sit outside and talk back and forth to each other across the street.[19]

We live in an old neighborhood. As we go for walks, we see closed-in porches — relics of a withered lifestyle. If porches exist today, they are tucked away in the backyard where we can enjoy our privacy and independence.

The fast pace of today's leisure crowds out fellowship. We rush to the gym during our lunch break for a quick game of racquetball, a shower, and then back to the office. There is no time for leisurely sipping a glass of iced tea while we catch up on a friend's life. In fact, we would probably feel guilty if we "wasted" time in casual conversation.

Furthermore, our primary form of leisure, television, has had a numbing effect on children's social development. Kids average an incredible twenty-eight hours each week in front of the tube. This passive use of time can be devastating to their social skills because it eats up the time they should be talking or even quarreling with others. Interaction while watching T.V. is pared to the essentials — "Pass the popcorn" or "Hey, that's my chair!"

Conclusion

When I was in junior high, some friends and I organized a scavenger hunt. We asked politely for eggs or tomatoes at one house and then impolitely pelted a house further down the block with the produce. We were obviously lacking in basic mental capacities. We were easily recognized by friends of our parents. Our parents were called and allowed to discipline our foolishness. But what would happen today? Because communities are less cohesive, we probably would not have been recognized. As a result, the police would have been called to judge our misdeeds.

The erosion of community life has increased the burden on families. In early America, families were *less* important than today because the community supported the home. Kids benefited from visits to the neighbors, community dances and celebrations, trips to town, and community work. Parents didn't worry about drugs or child molesters or pornographic material when their child ventured into the community.

In the next two chapters I will attempt to show how we can rebuild the ties with others — particularly the bonds within the immediate and extended family. Full Christian maturity will be impossible unless we are connected to a diversity of others. What role do we play in our children's development? What role do they play in ours? What function do grandparents and friends perform? What do we have to give to them? Everyone benefits from intergenerational family life.

9

RESTORING COMMUNITY: THE IMMEDIATE FAMILY

About all that can be said for television as a diversion for children is that it beats public executions, which they often witnessed in seventeenth-century England and France.[1]

In today's changing family scene, brothers and sisters not infrequently lend each other the help and protection they are failing to receive from their parents.[2]

The only way to be "filled to the measure of all the fullness of God" is to do it "together with all the saints" (see Ephesians 3:14–19). Maturity is developed through community.

Becoming a human being, wrestling our inarticulate hungers and possibilities into shape, . . . can only be accomplished by being surrounded by examples of that process in various stages of production—siblings and cousins both younger and older, grandparents left alone or in pairs, aunts and uncles either single or married, and especially

fathers and mothers. Not to live inside this animated gal-
lery of instructive models is to suffer deprivation so deep
that one's identity as a human becomes deformed or severely limited.[3]

This type of interplay among the generations will be a
characteristic of the Messianic age.

This is what the LORD Almighty says: "Once again men
and women of ripe old age will sit in the streets of Jerusa-
lem, each with cane in hand because of his age. The city
streets will be filled with boys and girls playing there."
(Zechariah 8:4–5)

But as seen in the last chapter, our culture undermines
the commitments that make intergenerational life possible.
One author advised those entering mid-life: "You are moving
away. Away from institutional claims and other people's
agenda. . . . You are moving out of roles and into the self. If I
could give everyone a gift for the send-off on this journey it
would be . . . the gift of portable roots."[4]

In contrast, these next two chapters will attempt to show
that the way to weather a mid-life crisis, or any crisis for that
matter, is through a commitment to our roots. The focus of
these chapters will be the contribution of the extended family
in developing Christian maturity.

The Role of Parents

This entire book deals with the impact of parents on their
children's progress toward Christian maturity. But there are
two roles that are not developed elsewhere.

Toward Their Children: Parents as Protectors

The world has become a less friendly place for children.
The profound social changes include:

the so-called sexual revolution, the women's movement, the proliferation of television, the rampant increase in divorce and single parenthood, . . . [and] a deteriorating economic situation that propels more mothers into the work force.[5]

Unfortunately, many parents look at society's turmoil and conclude that "children must be exposed early to adult experience in order to survive an increasingly complex and uncontrollable world."[6] We no longer think about *protecting* children, but *preparing* them. Thus, kids have been left with less nurturance at a time when they desperately need more.

God designed the home to be a sanctuary. He repeatedly reminded Israel to care for those without the protection of a home — widows, orphans, and aliens.

Eliot Daley, speaking from the child's perspective, explains the concept of sheltering:

It must be a comfortable feeling to know that someone is taking care of you, even in ways that may rankle for a while. A child must feel good to understand that a parent knows more than the child, and is stronger and wiser in some ways — competent to frame directions for growing.[7]

Sheltering, then, is "transmitting to children the sense that they are separate and special and under adults' careful supervision."[8]

Many parents today release their children before their defense systems are sound. Kids need protection from several foes.

Adult burdens. When our oldest boy was six years old, I led a family study on world hunger. I read a heart-wrenching story that included pictures of starving people. Nathan became extremely upset and begged me to remove the pictures. I was irritated. It wasn't the response I had envisioned! Some time later, we visited a home for the elderly. Nathan encountered a number of patients who were in physical and emotional pain. He begged to leave. Again, I was disappointed.

But now I understand. That information was too heavy for him. Now that he is a teenager, he has been joyfully volunteering at a retirement home.

Child psychologist David Elkind explains that there are intense pressures for children

> to grow up fast intellectually — to know more about the poor, the disabled, the sick, and emotionally troubled. But young children . . . have their own personal agenda, a need to make sense out of their own lives before they can fully appreciate the predicament of others.[9]

When young children are asked to study complex world problems or choose which school they should attend or help mom decide whether she should marry her boyfriend, they are being asked to carry unreasonable burdens.

Television. We have a solution for the parent who is wearied by a child's oft repeated: "I'm bored." When our boys complain of boredom, we tell them that it is like saying, "I'm stupid," because a creative person can devise endless ways to use their time. However, before we are too hard on our children, we should lay the blame where it mostly belongs — T.V.

The corrupting influence of television's content has been well-documented. However, an equal peril is T.V.'s tranquilizing effect on motivation and creativity. A married student with two children turned off his television for two weeks as part of a class assignment. He explained that the withdrawal pains were considerable — his wife initially visited a friend to watch her soap operas. But as the experiment progressed, puzzles and unused toys emerged from the closets. The family completed several dormant projects. Mom sewed again after years of idleness. The couple's sex life was invigorated.

During the early years of parenting, Cathy and I believed that after learning the basics of child-rearing, our household would be dominated by peace and harmony. CRASH! Our expectations slammed into reality. But that illusion should have been shattered. For it is in the resolution of conflict that we mature. When my wife and I battle over whether to drive six hundred miles to visit her family, I am confronted with my self-ish desire to avoid a long car trip. When a child has repeated conflicts with a sick sibling, he can learn to be gracious.

However, in many households the television has been used to mute discord.

> Instead of having to establish rules and limits, . . . parents could solve all these problems by resorting to the television set. "Go watch TV" were the magic words. Now mothers could cook dinner in peace, or prepare their briefs for the next day's case, or whatever. No need to work on training the children to play quietly while mothers and fathers discussed a family matter without interruption.[10]

Though television can be a peacemaker, its terms of peace are too costly. Children trained by it never learn self-control or understand the effort that is required to build relationships: "Be completely humble and gentle; be patient, bearing with one another in love. Make every effort to keep the unity of the Spirit through the bond of peace" (Ephesians 4:2–3).

Mom and Dad, you cannot control your child's T.V. habits until you control your own. Formerly, I was spending nearly two hours a day watching news-related programs. Now I depend on *Newsweek* for a more comprehensive and quicker view of current events. Parents, if you are watching more than an hour of T.V. per day, you are watching too much. There are more profitable ways to spend your time—personal Bible study, reading a book to a child, visiting a friend, exercising your body.

Music. Allan Bloom believes that "nothing is more singular about this generation [of children] than its addiction to music." As he explains:

Today, a very large proportion of young people . . . live for music. It is their passion; nothing else excites them as it does; they cannot take seriously anything alien to music. When they are in school and with their families, they are longing to plug themselves back into their music.[11]

The danger of music is similar to T.V. In addition to the immoral influence of its content, music can hinder the development of relationships. Listening to loud music destroys "shared speech [which] is the essence of friendship."[12]

Furthermore, kids need time to think and imagine. Many forms of modern music negate thought. If we want to protect our kids we must control not only the quality but the quantity of music they listen to.

Peer group. I am amazed at the notion that a child needs enormous amounts of time with his age-mates to become mature. If anything, the opposite is true. A study of teens found that those who were more peer-oriented than their friends were also more negative toward themselves and their future, rated their parents lower in affection and support, were involved in more delinquent behavior, and even viewed the peer group more negatively.[13] Another study found that daycare children were more aggressive, more impulsive, more hyperactive, more egocentric, and more self-assertive, but less cooperative and less impressed by punishment than children who stay at home.[14]

Most assume that the peer orientation of youth is normal. But traditionally, teens didn't balk at family outings. Nor were they embarrassed by their parents' company in public — a town dance included grandmothers, mothers, and granddaughters. Today, many home school families find that their kids are not ruled by the peer group. Our boys still let us drape an arm around them in public. They enjoy family outings. They often choose activities with aunts and uncles rather than their age-mates.

But what causes a peer-oriented child? It "is more a product of parental disregard than of the attractiveness of the peer group. . . . He turns to his age-mates less by choice than by default."[15] He is like a child reared on junk food — he believes his diet is more appetizing than nutritional food because he is seldom served the better fare.

Sociologist Urie Bronfenbrenner believes that if a child's diet is not enriched, it will become a problem of the "greatest magnitude":

> We cannot escape the conclusion that if the current trend persists, if the institutions in our society continue to remove parents, other adults, and older children from the active participation in the lives of the children, and if the resulting vacuum is filled by the age-segregated peer group, we can anticipate increased alienation, indifference, antagonism, and violence on the part of the younger generation in all segments of our society.[16]

Why does overexposure to the peer group corrupt children? Because children, who are still forming their own values, are inadequate models. This is true of all kids, even those in church or a Christian school. In spite of the fact that our boys have received Christ and that we have labored to direct their character, they are still frequently vengeful, jealous, quarrelsome, competitive, insensitive, and stingy. Children need to be surrounded by people who can love the unlovely, who can be calm when irritated, and who can insist that children don't ridicule others.

Because children cannot socialize other children, they must be sheltered from *excessive* contact with one another. As a result, we limit our boys to one sport at a time; they must choose one of the youth activities rather than going Wednesday, Friday, and Sunday evenings; they can invite a friend to sleep over, but the next day will be a family day. Even when our kids spend time with their peers, we remain involved—playing cards, swimming together, attending a movie.

Furthermore, because maturity is built through ample contact with mature adults, we plan activities with other adults. We vacation with other families. We share one evening a week with another family. We help plan church activities that integrate the ages.

Overprotectiveness. Parenting demands careful discernment. At what age should you allow a child to ride his bike around the block? to the store? across town to a friend's? How high should a four-year-old be permitted to climb in a tree? a six-year-old? a ten-year-old? At what age is a child ready to budget his money, his leisure, his study time? The line between protectiveness and overprotectiveness is murky.

Furthermore, an evolving view of protectiveness has complicated the problem. During my high school years, I was not allowed to go out on school nights, I had a strict curfew on weekends, I was not allowed to see certain movies, and I was required to attend most family functions. Overly strict parents? I didn't think so. Most of my friends had similar restrictions. But what formerly passed for good parenting may now be viewed as smothering a child.

Our eventual goal—to transfer our kids dependence from us to the Lord—is achieved gradually. In the interim, we will have to make some decisions which our kids don't have the maturity to make. But it can be difficult to hold to your convictions when most parents are hurrying their children toward maturity. You may become exhausted by your child whining, "But Dad, why not? Everyone in the whole world who is anybody is going to that party. You want me to be a reject?"

Unfortunately, in our fear of crippling our kids with overprotectiveness, many of us have abandoned our older kids. When Paul told the Ephesian elders that he was committing them "to God and to the word of his grace" (Acts 20:32), he was not relinquishing all future involvement. Releasing our kids to the Lord does not mean that they must be turned out of our homes on their eighteenth birthday. Unmarried adults lived with their parents in Biblical times. Nor does it mean that a child must move to another city to find employment. Nor does it mean that a parent cannot furnish the down payment on a child's home. Scripture calls for parents to support their adult children. For example, they are to be involved in the spiritual training of and provide an inheritance for their grandchildren. Parents who cut off support for their adult children may be loading them with unnecessary burdens.

But on the other hand, parents, children must suffer the consequences of wrong choices. If you attempt to bail them out of every predicament, you may be getting in the way of God's discipline. Knowing when to release a child to his own choices and when to protect him from bad choices makes all of us dependent on our heavenly Father for wisdom.

Conclusion. The fallout from rushing a child's independence is often difficult to detect, as a former latchkey child testified:

> Outwardly all seemed well: I made all A's on report cards, had abundant friends, was well-liked by both children and adults. . . .

> But I wandered through many days of those early years lonely to my very core. The universe was essentially a lonely place, and life was to be lived in a shadow, interspersed with bright moments. Gradually the feeling emerged as a question: Did anyone really care? . . .[17]

But the results of hurrying cannot be hidden forever.

> [As this child] grows older, true maturity, defined by an ability to share, to empathize, to sacrifice, to be generous, to love unselfishly, and to nurture and care for children of his own, may prove elusive, and in its place attention seek-

ing and narcissism become the characteristics that define his adult life.[18]

When we push children out of the nest too soon, we may cause them to "cling to childhood longer, perhaps all their lives."[19]

Toward Their Children: Parents as Authorities.

Many parents today are more concerned about being liked than obeyed. But Scripture has a different emphasis: "Children, obey your parents" (Ephesians 6:1). Kids need to have an authority, not so much a friend, to guide them to maturity. They need someone who will stand firm when they can't be firm or don't understand the need for inflexibility.

> You can sometimes help a child more by denying him something—at the right time, in the right way—than by avoiding the occasion for the denial. How can parents bent on avoiding any occasion for disagreement, any denial of easy instant gratification, help a child learn self-control?[20]

If your goal is popularity, don't become a parent! You will not be appreciated when you censor your kids' movies—"But all the kids have seen it."—or when you restrict their parties—"But Jim's parents let him go."—or when you control their T.V.—"What's wrong with this program?" They may not understand why you establish a curfew—"Don't you trust me?"—or why they must attend a family picnic—"It will be borrrr-ing."—or why Sunday evening is reserved for the family—"You never let me do anything."

This barrage of opposition can be wearying. Our logic can be flawless, but our kids can't or won't agree. But what should we expect? "Folly is bound in the heart of the child," and it takes discipline to drive it from him.

The flip side of authority is respect—"Honor your father and mother . . . that it may go well with you and that you may enjoy long life on the earth" (Ephesians 6:2–3). Our goal is not mere compliance; we want our kids' esteem.

But our use of authority shapes our children's attitudes. As Saul was leading the Israelites in battle, he issued a thoughtless command: "Cursed be any man who eats food before evening comes, before I have avenged myself on my enemies" (see 1 Samuel 14).

Saul's son, Jonathan, who unknowingly ate during the day, quickly recognized his father's error: "My father has made trouble for the country. . . . How much better it would have been if the men had eaten today some of the plunder they took from their enemies. Would not the slaughter of the Philistines have been even greater?" (Children can always taste "the blood of arbitrariness leaking from a [parent's] wounded position!")[21]

But Saul wouldn't admit his error—in fact, he was prepared to put his son to death for disobeying his command! If we are unwilling to admit when our demands are off key— "You're right. There is no good reason why you can't spend the night at Chris' "—we will undermine our children's respect for us.

Furthermore, we encourage respect when we major on majors. When Peter rebuked Jesus for talk about death on the cross, fire blazed in Jesus' eyes: "Out of my sight, Satan! You are a stumbling block to me" (Matthew 16:23). However, when Jesus' disciples were arguing about which one of them was the greatest, He quietly gathered them to Himself and said, "Whoever wants to become great among you must be your servant" (Mark 10:43). Some situations call for a sharp rebuke, others call for a gentle reminder, still others call for silence.

One summer my boys brought a friend on a weekend fishing trip. While exploring the shoreline, they discovered a mud pit. Wearing only their swimsuits, they began jumping and rolling in the slimy, sticky mud. It was not my idea of fun, but they were electrified. My first thought was to deny their pleasure, but I couldn't manufacture a reason. My only advice was to not leap into the pit, as it might hold hidden rocks. A few minutes later, the friend, who had ignored my counsel, flew feet first into the goo and scraped his leg on a sharp stick. It wasn't serious, but he looked at me like: "Hey, you do know what you are talking about." When we limit our "no's" to the essentials, it will be easier for our kids to respect us.

But what are the essentials? Are hairstyles, clothing, spotless rooms, or table manners worth major confrontations? Probably not. On the other hand, movies, dating, work habits, and sibling relationships certainly are majors. We will inevitably fight with our children — we need to pick our fights carefully.

Finally, respect can be destroyed by unrealistic expectations. Cathy and I realize that we sometimes expect our boys to behave more consistently than we do ourselves. For example, if Cathy wants something fixed, she may have to remind me repeatedly. It isn't that I have bad intentions — I simply get easily distracted. The two of us often chuckle over my absentmindedness. But if we ask one of our kids to perform a task, and they get distracted — WATCH OUT!

Parents, don't delay establishing your authority. It is easier (note: I didn't say easy, but easier!) to teach a two-year-old not to throw food than convince an out-of-control teenager that he must be careful who he dates.

Toward Their Parents

God's word reminds us that we must care for those who have nurtured us.

> If a widow has children or grandchildren, these should learn first of all to put their religion into practice by caring for their own family and so repaying their parents and grandparents, for this is pleasing to God. (1 Timothy 5:3–4)

The commitment to our parents will take various forms. I accepted part-time work in my father's business as a way of "repaying" him. The company was being reorganized, with dad reducing his daily involvement. I thought that my people skills could be used in the transition.

Others may respond to God's command by inviting an aging parent to live with them. Another might view God's best as a nursing home with medical care. Others may be led to move closer to mom and dad. The choices can be agonizing:

> Would I be able to keep [Mom] with us, or would I have to put her in a "home" — what an obscene misuse of a word! Homes for the aged, nursing homes, are one of the horrors of our time, but for many people there is no alternative. . . . There are still those who think my mother should be put away. Put away. Everything in me revolts at the thought. But my belief that we are supposed to share all of life with each other, dying and decay as well as feasting and fun, is being put to the test.[22]

Jesus rebuked the Pharisees for slithering out of their responsibility to their parents. Therefore, we must ask God *seriously* what we can give to those who have given so much to us.

The Role of Children

Toward Their Parents

Jesus instructed His disciples to become servants — and children are specialists in teaching servanthood! They teach us how to love when wronged, to react calmly to conflict, to discern the unspoken needs of others, to comfort the hurting (and those who think they are hurting!), and to be patient with the immature. Children are truly a "heritage," a "reward" from God (see Psalms 127:3). Parents who forsake their role are losing an opportunity that many "have never had before and, once [their] children are grown, may never have again."

Furthermore, my kids add color to my heavenly sonship. Because of the love that I have for my sons, I now have a deeper understanding of God's love for me. I now appreciate a Father who meets my unrecognized needs. I have a glimpse of God's patience, while He waits for me to mature.

Close friends of ours have a fourteen-year-old autistic son. Though he lived in their home for seven years, though they have served him under great duress, though they have sacrificed their comfort and their shame, he still does not know them. There are no shouted greetings: "I'm home, Mom!" There are no enthusiastic pronouncements: "I scored a goal, Dad!" There are no professions of love, "I love you Mommy." However, these parents empathize, in a way that few can, with God's pain when His children don't acknowledge Him.

Toward Their Grandparents

It doesn't take much insight to recognize that "children's children are a crown to the aged" (Proverbs 17:6). Bumper stickers that read: "Ask Me About My Grandchildren," and photo-packing grandparents are modern testimonies to the enthusiasm of grandparents for their grandchildren. One grandfather explained:

> I think I actually enjoy my grandchildren more than I did my own children. [Because] I don't have the full responsibility for my grandchildren. . . . What's even greater, we can enjoy the children for a day or a weekend or a week and then give them back to their parents. Wonderful! Kids for rent, and no charge![23]

Being a grandparent imparts a sense of need to many elderly. An anxious, new mother turns to her mother to teach her how to care for a newborn. A teenager asks his grandparents to mediate a conflict with his parents. Grandparents watch the kids for a weekend — which is greeted by the kids

with as much enthusiasm as a trip to an amusement park —
while the parents enjoy a respite.

Toward Siblings

All of our boys enjoy playing board games — what else can
you do during South Dakota's long winters? — and Monopoly
is one of their favorites. When they began playing, Jered was
still a preschooler. Mimicking his older brothers, he would roll
the dice (often out of turn), move his marker to the position
of his choice, draw money from the bank, "purchase" property, and place hotels on property that was not his. At first,
they were frustrated by the disruption, but eventually they
learned to endure and even laugh at the antics of their little
brother.

During my childhood, kids were ridiculed for having
younger friends. What a shame! Mixed age groups have more
nurturance, helping, cooperation, protectiveness, and sharing,
but less aggression and competition. To help our boys enjoy
the benefits of mixing the ages, we don't let them exclude
their brothers all or even most of the time when a friend visits. As a result, they share many of the same friends. Furthermore, we encourage our children to babysit. And when we
vacation with other families, we aren't concerned about
matching the ages of children.

Segregation of the ages has made it difficult for new parents to be prepared for parenting. If Cathy's and my childhood had included more exposure to babies, the initial night
our firstborn was home, we certainly would not have set the
alarm to awaken us for his next feeding!

Conclusion

The family was designed by God to frame our identity:

I had never heard the term "identity crisis" until after I was
fifty. Very early I knew who I was. My father, though kind,
never let me forget that I was under his authority and care

as his son. My four brothers and sister, in one way or another, reminded me that I belonged to them. Sunday after Sunday in church I was told that I was a child of God, whatever terror or comfort that might bring. In any event, I knew who I was, son, brother, child of God.[24]

Many moderns are lost. Returning to their roots may help them find their way.

10

RESTORING COMMUNITY: THE EXTENDED FAMILY

[Extended] family members are the people you don't have to work to impress. You can be yourself. There's no test to pass, no fee to belong. You have a right to be included simply because you are.[1]

S trong families will only be achieved in concert with others—"Though one may be overpowered, two can defend themselves. A cord of three strands is not quickly broken" (Ecclesiastes 4:12). God designed the extended family to be one of the primary supports for families.

The Role of Grandparents

Toward Their Grandchildren

Our culture belittles the role of grandparents. Recently, the U.S. Department of Health and Welfare interviewed senior citizens to assess their needs. Not one of the questions

used in the four-hour interview permitted the elderly to discuss how grandchildren might fit into a fuller life![2]

But the Bible informs us that part of a grandparent's fulfillment comes from nurturing grandchildren. They are commanded to share God's word (see Deuteronomy 4:9) and their
inheritance with their grandchildren (see Proverbs 13:22).

The need for grandparents. The functions that God designed grandparents to fulfill have not disappeared. They
have simply "been taken over by surrogates which have no
personal, lasting or emotional commitment to children." Psychologist Arthur Kornhaber summarized the changes:[3]

Functions of Grandparents	Institutionalized Replacements
Feeders (Sunday dinner at Grandmother's house)	Restaurants; fast-food outlets; junk food
Caretakers	Baby-sitters; day-care centers; schools; medical professionals; jail; television
Negotiators (between child and parents)	Child's peer group; family and personal therapists; experts on childrearing
Mentors	Schoolteachers; television; peers; rock stars and other celebrities; cults
Role models	Media stereotypes of elders; no-body
Connections with the past	Television; movies; family albums; parental memories

My boys choose grandma's cooking over their favorite restaurant. Why? Because the food is better? The food is good—but

not that good. At grandma's house, they receive more than physical nourishment.

Grandparents offer their grandkids an "emotional sanctuary from the pressures of the world."[4] They don't make kids eat their peas. They don't enforce due dates on term papers. They aren't teaching them how to use money responsibly. (In fact, grandparents' lavish gifts seem designed to teach just the opposite!) Kids thrive on the gracious love of grandparents.

Furthermore, grandparents add stability to children's lives by reciting family history—stories of "the way it used to be." My boys are enchanted by their grandpa's stories. One of their favorites recounts a younger brother shooting himself in the foot, while their parents were enjoying the only vacation they ever took. Their interlude was interrupted with the terse telegram: "OZZIE SHOT HIMSELF." They dashed home, not knowing whether he was dead or alive, maimed or okay. No wonder they never vacationed again! But are such stories merely idle tales? No. They give children a sense of roots, of belonging to "history, not just to the temporary and fluctuating scene."

Additionally, grandparents help kids develop positive attitudes toward old age and the elderly. One study discovered that kids who had minimal contact with their grandparents

> derided elders as being "too old" and "out of touch," "the kinds of people they did not want to be like." They saw no reason to turn to older people for advice. . . . Finally these youngsters had little knowledge of how they would be and act when they were their grandparents' age. On the contrary, they found it difficult, even annoying, to discuss their own future as "old people."[5]

Grandfathers are particularly needed. Most children are raised by women—moms, day-care centers, schools. So granddads have an opportunity to fill the child's need for male role models.

Finally, the words of a seven-year-old may best summarize the role of grandparents:[6]

WHAT A GRANDMOTHER IS

A grandmother is a lady who has no children of her own. She likes other people's little girls. A grandfather is a man grandmother. He goes for walks with the boys, and they talk about fishing and tractors and like that.

Grandmas don't have to do anything except be there. They're old, so they shouldn't play hard or run. It is enough if they drive us to the market where the pretend horse is and have lots of dimes ready. Or, if they take us for walks, they should slow down past things like pretty leaves or caterpillars. They should never say, "Hurry up."

Usually, they are fat but not too fat to tie your shoes. They wear glasses and funny underwear. They can take their teeth and gums off. . . . They don't have to be smart, only answer questions like what makes flowers grow.

Everybody should try to have one, especially if you don't have television, because Grandmas are the only grownups who have got time.

Greater opportunity for grandparents. Grandparents can fulfill their role better today than ever before. Consider the modern advantages:[7]

- fewer grandchildren permits them to spend more time with each one.

- earlier retirement.

- better physical health.

- greater financial security.

- longer life expectancy.

- easier to visit because of modern transportation.

But these gains have seldom translated into greater commitments to grandchildren.

Greater obstacles for grandparents. Some parents restrict their children's time with their grandparents, believing these grandparents were inadequate parents. But many parents become better nurturers when they become grandparents. Shortly after I moved back to South Dakota, my dad invited me to hear him speak at a local banquet. I wasn't planning to accept, but his persistent requests changed my mind. During the speech he told a few anecdotes about his grandsons. Then, glancing in my direction, he added: "I guess I spend so much time with them because I wasn't around much when their dad was growing up." My dad is a better grandparent than he was a father—he takes the boys to breakfast most Saturdays; they attend the State Fair together; they share work at his farm; they hunt and fish together. I have no regrets. I am thankful for his commitment to my sons.

However, the psychoanalytic theories of family life may have had the most dampening affect on grandparent/grandkid ties. That philosophy believes that unless:

> young couples, upon their marriage, [do] not separate themselves effectively from their parents, they [will] experience disturbed relationships between themselves and also have trouble bringing up healthy children.[8]

This viewpoint is so pervasive today that interviewers of over five hundred grandparents heard repeatedly "that good grandparents should not 'interfere' in their children's lives, especially with regard to how the children were raising the grandchildren."[9]

Finally, intimacy between some grandparents and their grandkids has been hindered by a selfish, deceptive desire for independence. One grandfather was asked if he was bothered by living a long distance from his grandchildren:

> Bother me? Absolutely not. That's the best thing about it. We only see them at Christmas. And that's the way I like it. I don't want to get too involved in raising my grandchildren. It was enough blood, sweat, and tears getting my own children raised. I don't want to go through it again with my grandchildren.[10]

Many grandparents are more committed to their leisure than to their grandchildren. Though there is a place for travel and entertainment, many retirees have forgotten that true life is found in serving others. When Paul instructed us "to do good, to be rich in good deeds, and to be generous and willing to share," he commended a sacrificial life so that we can "take hold of the life that is truly life" (see 1 Timothy 6:17–21).

Toward Their Children

Archaeologists have unearthed a new version of the Prodigal Son in which the father acts more responsibly toward his grown son. Rather than wrapping his arms around his wayward boy, he is more cautious, demanding an explanation of the boy's wanton behavior. Rather than calling for a festive celebration, he asks the young man to meditate on his errors. Rather than restoring the squanderer to his position within the family, he makes him prove himself by working on the estate.

You may be asking, where did that version come from? It could have been edited by many modern day family therapists who worry that the gracious support of a parent will cripple a grown child.

But as we have seen, parental responsibility does not stop when a child leaves home. One Christian author advised that a parent should leave his inheritance to charity, not his children. But God's word views inheritance from a parent as natural—"Houses and wealth are inherited from parents" (Proverbs 19:14). Our view of having kids stand on their own two feet may reflect more of an American Frontier philosophy than Biblical truth.

Grandparents will not enfeeble their adult children if they send an occasional check or offer advice on parenting. When will we wake up? Grandparents have so much to share:

> I try to talk to the kids about this work thing, about how it made me miss out on all of the birthday parties and important events in the family and I don't think I'm getting through. It seems that the young people are more workaholic than I was. I could teach them something important, but they don't listen.[11]

Greater intimacy between parents and their grown kids will spark conflicts. When grandparents want to lavish sweets or money on our kids, we may object. When grandparents criticize our parenting skills, we may be hurt. When they want to give us money, we may resent their assistance. However, "conflicts are unavoidable in close relationships. But remember that the success of a relationship should not be judged by the amount of conflict or disagreement, but by the way you handle it."[12]

The Role of Extended Family

It is confounding. My California sister and her kids journey to South Dakota every summer for two to three weeks. We have no beach, no Disneylands, no professional sports; and the kids have no one their age to play with. So why do they come? They come to enjoy the sanctuary of extended family. Here they can relax in a love that isn't based on their athletic skills or the shape of their bodies or their G.P.A.

One must have something in this world to take for granted — or "granite" as children sometimes say — and [my extended family is] my granite, my bedrock. This original family of mine provides me with a broad and steady base to stretch out on.[13]

Toward Children

One of our sons had difficulty finding a "best friend" as a preteen. One day when he was playing at another boy's house, he was ordered to leave because the boy wanted to play with someone else. Afterward, our son hid and cried in our back closet — too ashamed to talk about his rejection. Though Cathy and I tried to bolster his confidence in building a friendship, it was his uncle Paul who had the greatest influence. While enjoying lunch together, he learned that Paul didn't have a close friend until college. Our son was shocked. How could someone as attractive as his uncle have trouble finding a friend? The next few times they were alone, he asked about Paul's childhood friendships. Those conversations were a turning point — our boy discerned that finding a friend may not be related to his own worthiness. As a result, he became more aggressive in finding a friend. He now has several. The extended family is certainly "the best soil in which children have the opportunity to grow up to be emotionally healthy and altruistic adults."[14]

Toward Adults

But the extended family is not just for the young. After fleeing Egypt, Moses found a haven in Midian where he married the daughter of Jethro. For forty years, he tended his father-in-law's flocks while living within a large clan (Jethro had seven daughters). Those relationships were vital to Moses throughout his life. While mediating the deliverance from Egypt, his family was sheltered in Midian. While traveling to Canaan, Jethro advised an exhausted Moses to delegate his responsibilities—advice which may have prevented an emotional breakdown.

Staying close to one's roots may mean the difference between spiritual vitality and spiritual decay. One study found that those who relocate frequently are more prone to divorce than those who are stable.[15]

Living in my home town has been a boon to my growth: I have enjoyed emotional and financial support from my parents; I have felt secure when people recognize the family name; I have had the assurance that if I fail as a writer, I can find employment with family or friends; I was asked to teach at a local college largely because I was known; I have had the encouragement of friends and relatives when the church that I was pastoring dissolved. During our years in Sioux Falls, I have frequently been asked to relocate and join thriving ministries. And the requests often came when I was most discouraged about ministry here. But as I evaluated, I realized that leaving would have meant leaving many God-given responsibilities. Not only has God called me to be a teacher and a shepherd, but I am also a husband, a friend, a neighbor, a brother, a nephew, a cousin, a coach, a board member, a son, a father. We chose to stay in large part because leaving Sioux Falls would have forced us to withdraw from a broad tapestry of relationships.

The Role of the Community

In earlier America, the community and the home complemented each other. Visits to the neighbors, trips to town, and community work allowed kids to relate to a host of adults who shared the home's values. When I was a boy, an elderly woman in my neighborhood introduced me to the delights of Winnie-the-Pooh. Another neighbor stocked his freezer with popsicles for us kids.

But the community is no longer an ally. Neighborhoods and schools are not safe. Rock music and peer pressure advocate irresponsible sex. Television and magazines alluringly package the way of death. In a teen magazine, an article on virginity included questions teens might be afraid to ask— "Should I talk during sex?" "Will it hurt?" "How long will it take?"[16] An article on virginity? Hardly. It was an article on how to lose your virginity.

When society degenerates, the home is saddled with a greater burden. But parents can't do the job on their own.

> Two are better than one, because they have a good return for their work: If one falls down, his friend can help him up. But pity the man who falls and has no one to help him up! (Ecclesiastes 4:9–10)

Parents, your family won't find God's fullness until you open your lives to others. But the profound obstacles to community—harried lifestyles, mobility, work that separates families and friends, desire for freedom—make significant relationships an arduous task.

How then can families rebuild community? Vacation with other families. Meet with another family one night a week for fun, worship, and fellowship. Participate in appropriate community activities—Easter services, crusades, picnics, parades, political debates, or a community fund drive.

Unfortunately, many adults assume that children hinder adult fun. Recently I served on a committee to plan our twenty-year high school reunion. At my suggestion, we planned a family picnic for Saturday afternoon. We ate, played softball, reminisced. Most agreed that it was the highlight of the weekend.

Finally, since building community is a lengthy project, we may need to follow the example of Eliot Daley. "When the cultural tide started sucking [his family] out of port once more,"—they planned to move to a new city—he declared:

Enough moving. Here we had just left one more set of friends we loved, and by whom we felt loved. . . . These were people we wanted for lifelong friends. We did not want them, too, to slip into the nether world of fading faces lost to us except once a year, at Christmas-time, when a token is exchanged symbolizing the residue of a relationship.[17]

Commitment to the Lord and to Roots

But doesn't God's Word encourage us to leave our homes and our families to follow Christ? When Peter reminded Jesus that he had left everything to follow Him, he was praised:

I tell you the truth, . . . no one who has left home or brothers or sisters or mother or father or children or fields for me and the gospel will fail to receive a hundred times as much in this present age (homes, brothers, sisters, mothers, children and fields — and with them, persecutions) and in the age to come, eternal life. (Mark 10:29–30)

At times, God will uproot us for the sake of the gospel. But the Biblical norm is living close to one's roots. The itinerant ministry of the early church was carried on primarily by single men. In Mark 5:19, after healing the Gerasene demoniac, Jesus instructed the man: "Go home to your family and tell them how much the Lord has done for you." (When have you heard a missionary call to go home?) In the New Testament letters to the churches, not once are believers encouraged to forsake their homes to follow Christ. The emphasis is on how to live within their communities. God calls us to be obedient children, loving parents, faithful workers, respectful citizens, light-bearing Christians, hospitable neighbors. When Jesus spoke about a ripe harvest, He wasn't pleading with us to go somewhere, simply to become harvesters.

Conclusion

A commitment to intergenerational family life may not be very glamorous. In the movie, *Nothing In Common*, Jackie Gleason was an emotionally and physically hurting father whose son (Tom Hanks) was a rising advertising executive. This needy father was an irritant to his busy son — calling him at work, dropping by the office, asking him to run his errands. However, when a client demanded that the son go to New York at a time when his father was in critical condition in the hospital, the son refused. The client was incredulous: "Doesn't he have good doctors?" But the son stood firm, awakening to the fact that his father's need for comfort was greater than his need for business success.

As the movie demonstrated, both givers and receivers benefit. The father needed his son's support. But the son needed his father to renew his sense of priorities.

In our fractured world, not everyone can go or stay home. A friend's parents were divorced after he left home. Neither parent now lives in his home town. One of them is remarried, and he feels like a stranger when he visits. But that doesn't decrease his need for a home. That is why Jesus, while hanging on the cross, asked John to take His mother into his care. God's word frequently reminds us to shelter orphans, widows, and foreigners.

We live in an imperfect world. All grandparents, aunts and uncles, cousins have warts. But does God's Word call us to care only for the lovely? the mature? those who know Christ? No. Giving to family is not an option. "If anyone does not provide for his relatives, and especially for his immediate family, he has denied the faith and is worse than an unbeliever" (1 Timothy 5:8). The way each of us apply this truth may vary, but apply it we must.

PART FOUR

SPIRITUAL TRAINING

11

LAYING THE FOUNDATION

One generation will commend
your works to another;
they will tell of your mighty acts.

(Psalms 145:4)

God's people have frequently faltered in transmitting the faith. When Joshua's generation was dead, the author of Judges declared:

> The people served the LORD throughout the lifetime of Joshua and of the elders who outlived him and who had seen all the great things the LORD had done for Israel. . . . [But] after that whole generation had been gathered to their fathers, another generation grew up, who knew neither the LORD nor what he had done for Israel. (2:7, 10)

Nurturing our children's faith—never an easy task—has been complicated by our culture's increasing hostility to Truth. Recently, *Mad*, a satirical magazine for teens, included a parody of *Little Darlings*—a film about two young girls at summer camp racing to lose their virginity. *Mad's* sketch depicted "an outdoor salesman hawking: 'Get your training diaphragms here,'" and a girl spying on a couple and reporting, "She's starting foreplay now."[1] However, the most shocking feature of this article may be that the concepts are understood by *Mad's* readership, whose average age is thirteen. When I was thirteen, I would have guessed that foreplay was something that kids did before serious play!

It isn't just deteriorating morals, though, that hinder the transplanting of parental faith. Upheavals in our culture, which have been discussed earlier, have also influenced the spiritual development of the family.

The Transformation of Worship

A Family Setting

The Puritans, though a minority, became a model for many Americans in their commitment to Christian education in the home. They believed:

> Parents who cared only for the bodies of their children were neglectful of what was most important. . . . Every day the Bible was read and God was worshiped. . . . Parental obligations to children were enforced by law; if, after being warned, parents did not provide instruction in the home, their children might be taken from them and placed under such masters as the civil officials thought suitable.[2]

If parents were being prosecuted today for neglecting family worship, they would be in grave danger! However, it is seldom a question of ill intent. Parents simply can't generate the confidence or the time to transmit truth to their kids. As a result, they rely on the church, Christian schools, and youth ministries to stimulate and feed their children's spirituality.

However, when the home forfeits its role, negative influences dominate. One study found that only one in seven teenagers learned about sex at home. Who instructed the others? T.V. was their primary tutor! And what is T.V.'s curriculum? The average child views nearly ten thousand "sexually suggestive comments or scenes of sexual intercourse" each year.[3] And only one in five of those scenes portrays sex between married couples.[4] The survey found that the second largest source of teens' information about sex was their friends. If we don't pass on God's values to our children, they will ingest them from T.V. and other immature teens.

Furthermore, when parents surrender the training of their children to others, they lose touch with kids' capabilities. I received a letter from friends a few years ago which described their eleven-year-old as "completely dedicated to the Lord" and "a hungry student of the Scripture." But rates of maturation make this unlikely. Few eleven-year-olds have the physical hardware to be "completely dedicated." Spiritual maturity, like physical maturity, develops with age.

An Intergenerational Setting

A repeated theme of this book is that adult nurturance of children has diminished, largely because they are seldom together. The church is no exception — age-graded Sunday school classes, summer camps, vacation Bible schools, and youth groups parallel cultural tendencies to segregate kids and adults. The result is that many young people go "through high school without ever having had an opportunity . . . to sense their oneness with an intergenerational body of believers. Their church experience is homogeneous, graded first as pre-school, then primary, then junior."[5]

But God intended the generations to be united in worship. When Moses called the Israelites to worship, he instructed the people: "Assemble the people — men, women and children, and the aliens living in your towns — so that they can listen and learn to fear the LORD" (Deuteronomy 31:12). When Jesus spoke to the multitudes, He gathered children in

His arms. When Paul wrote letters to churches, children were addressed as part of the worshipping community.

A Leisurely Setting

In traditional culture, worship was not something squeezed into a cramped schedule. New Englanders were "horse shedders"—between the Sunday morning and late afternoon worship service they discussed political, religious, and social issues in the horse shed. The original Thanksgiving was a three-day celebration as the pilgrims and their Indian friends feasted, listened to prayers and sermons, sang songs of praise. They leisurely rejoiced in the abundant harvest which followed that first, killing winter.

The Biblical pace of worship was also relaxed. In the Old Testament, Israel's calendar set aside entire weeks for worshipping God. While the Apostle Paul was leading a late night Bible study, one of the participants fell to his death from a third-story window. The worship adjourned while Paul raised the young man back to life. Then they returned to their study until daybreak! (see Acts 20:7–12).

But we modern worshipers begin to fidget if church runs five minutes overtime. Few of us will give up a weekend, or even a day, for a retreat. We are uncomfortable when asked to be contemplative. We would much rather be *doing* something. Martha, not Mary, is our patron saint![6]

Christians are the elite of a harried people. Because we are conscientious workers, we work overtime. Because we are faithful parents, we attend all of our children's sporting events. Because we are loyal church members, we serve on several committees and teach a Sunday school class. Because we are concerned citizens, we serve on the board of the YMCA. No wonder worship has become tightly regimented.

If we intend to pass on a vital faith to our kids, these cultural trends must be countered.

The Role of the Home

The Goal

Jesus challenged His followers: "Love the Lord your God with *all* your heart and with *all* your soul and with *all* your mind and with *all* your strength" (Mark 12:30, emphasis added). But Christian parents often settle for far less. They are content if their kids attend church, avoid sex and drugs, marry a Christian. Our kids will never love and serve God wholeheartedly unless we do the same.

The Foundation

Moses' primer on passing the faith onto children begins with a focus on parents: "Love the LORD your God with all your heart and with all your soul and with all your strength" (Deuteronomy 6:5). Parental faith is the seed of children's faith.

It has been tempting for parents to substitute Christian activity for a relationship with God. Loving God may include serving on a church committee or teaching a Sunday school class, but it can never replace it. Loving God must always be a growing relationship of trust, obedience, prayer.

It begins in the heart. How is this consuming love achieved? Moses explained: "These commandments that I give you today are to be *upon your hearts*" (Deuteronomy 6:6, emphasis added). Parents will love that which they treasure, dream about, ponder. If they feed on *House Beautiful*, they will prize a well-designed and furnished home. If financial magazines are their delight, then making money will be their passion. On the other hand, if they treat God's laws as "more precious than gold, than much pure gold" (see Psalms 19:10), they will develop a heart for God.

Recently, I anticipated earning a substantial sum of money. My first thought was: "At last, I can junk my old car." (The two wedged-in golf tees holding up the driver's window are symbolic of the entire car's condition!) During the next few weeks I toyed with other dreams — a new home, travel to exotic places, an updated computer. At first, the thoughts were merely a playful diversion. But the more I entertained them, the more they controlled me. Finally, to free myself from these self-dominated dreams, I forced myself to dream about using the money to help others. I also reminded myself that I am already wealthy, being blessed with "every spiritual blessing in Christ" (see Ephesians 1:3). And I remembered that possessing Jesus, not material things, is the route to a satisfying life: "I have come that they may have life, and have it to the full" (John 10:10).

It takes obedience. As a young Christian, I agonizingly searched for the secret to the Christian life. Books enticed me such as *Hudson Taylor's Spiritual Secret* and *The Christian's Secret of a Happy Life.* Other Christians assured me that the "filling of the Holy Spirit" or "being baptized in the Spirit" or "speaking in tongues" would be the key that would unlock spiritual treasure. But there is no special knowledge or overwhelming experience that will ensure spiritual vitality. Moses explained what produces life:

> Now what I am commanding you today is not too difficult for you or beyond your reach. It is not up in heaven, so that you have to ask, "Who will ascend into heaven to get it and proclaim it to us so we may obey it?" Nor is it beyond the sea, so that you have to ask, "Who will cross the sea to get it and proclaim it to us so we may obey it?" No, the word is very near you; it is in your mouth and in your heart so you may obey it. (Deuteronomy 30:11–14)

The crux of the Christian life is obedience to God's accessible Word. We don't have to scale mountains or navigate seas to find it. His Word is "very near you; it is in your mouth and in your heart so you may obey it."

Parents, you have a choice between "life and prosperity, death and destruction." If you choose "to walk in [God's] ways, and to keep his commands, decrees and laws; then you will live and increase" (Deuteronomy 30:15–16). Do you want a home dominated by love, joy, peace, patience, goodness, kindness? Do you want your children to be devoted to their Heavenly Father? Then you must *diligently* obey His Word.

It takes time. Cathy and I have a marvelous relationship. We chat with each other for a few minutes at mealtime. Most evenings we talk in bed for a few moments before dozing off. We get along so well that we don't even need an occasional date or a weekend to ourselves. Sound realistic? Hardly. Yet many Christians attempt to build a relationship with God similarly. A relationship with God will *never, never, never* have any depth until a person gives God significant time in his daily, weekly, and yearly schedules.

Unfortunately, many of us are professional procrastinators:

The child is playing, he hasn't time right now . . . Later on . . .
The schoolboy has his homework to do, he hasn't time . . . Later on . . .
The young man is at his sports, he hasn't time . . . Later on . . .
The young married man has his new house, he has to fix it up, he hasn't time . . . Later on . . .
The grandparents have their grandchildren, they haven't time . . . Later on . . .
They are ill, they have their treatments, they haven't time . . . Later on . . .
They are dying, they have no . . .
Too late! . . . They have no more time![7]

A day of accounting is coming: "For we must all appear before the judgment seat of Christ, that each one may receive what is due him for the things done while in the body, whether good or bad" (2 Corinthians 5:10). Excuses won't do—"But Lord, I just didn't have time to . . ." The urgent must be controlled so that it doesn't trample the eternal.

Learning to say "yes". We make time for what we treasure. How many of us miss meals? We may postpone them, but we still eat. We find time to read the paper, to watch the news, to exercise our bodies. We must learn to say "yes" to what God values most.

Saying "yes" to God's priorities can be accomplished by discerning His will. When I know that God has commanded me to put Him first, when I understand my obligations as a father, a husband, and a son, when my gifts and ministry are defined, I can make good decisions about the use of my time.

You won't earn community awards for teaching God's Word to your kids, for scheduling time to pray, for staying home to study your Bible. You won't be eulogized for resigning from a committee that interferes with serving a Sunday school class. In fact, if you say "no" often enough to be faithful to God's demands, you may be criticized for not carrying your share of the burden in your church or your job or your community.

Conclusion

Commitments to God's priorities must be carefully monitored. Moses warned parents who had begun well:

> Only be careful, and watch yourselves closely so that you do not forget the things your eyes have seen or let them slip from your heart as long as you live. Teach them to your children and to their children after them. (Deuteronomy 4:9)

Live lobster should be boiled in a pot of initially cold water. The lobster, in spite of an increasingly hostile environment, will be tranquilized by the gradual temperature change.

But if the lobster is dropped into boiling water, watch out! He will thrash wildly, creating an unwelcome mess. Like the lobster, parents can be lulled from spiritual health. Few face dramatic temptations—invitations to commit adultery, opportunities to rob a bank. Instead, the subtle Enemy kills his prey by the small, daily choices—whether to read the Bible or watch T.V., whether to visit a lonely neig(bor or wax your car, whether to spend time with a daughter or play golf. Little by little, more and more frequently, choices are made to serve self, rather than God. One day a person finds he has been soothed into spiritual decay. He still attends church, sings in the choir, mouths Christian concepts, but there is no life within.

Parents, it is too easy to drift away from a vital relationship with Jesus Christ. Wake up before the pot boils! If you want your children to adopt heavenly values, then those values must be transforming your life.

12

PASSING ON THE FAITH

The Lord's Prayer we mumbled in grade school affected us less than the Pledge of Allegiance. . . . It was the home — and the houses of worship related to it — where religion lived.

Allan Bloom

The spiritual life of most homes is appalling:

The dreariness of the family's spiritual landscape passes belief. It is as monochrome and unrelated to those who pass through it as are the barren steppes frequented by nomads who take their mere subsistence and move on.[1]

Many of us parents recognize our failure in communicating truth to our kids, but excuse ourselves with: "I'm just not qualified to teach my children spiritual truth." Of course we aren't qualified! But were we skilled students our first day of kindergarten? Were we proficient parents the day we brought our first baby home? Competence grows through commitment and experience.

The Role of Parents

The godliness of a parent won't always be transmitted to his children. Even though King David was described as a man after God's heart, one of his sons attempted to seize his father's throne, and another son's sins eventually split the kingdom.

How then is truth relayed? Paul explained to the Philippians: "Whatever you have learned or received or heard from me, or seen in me — put it into practice" (Philippians 4:9). Paul told the Philippians to practice what they had seen (*modeling*) and heard (*teaching*) from him. We influence our kids by our deeds and our words.

Modeling

While driving, a dad comments: "Wow! Look at that 'Vet. What I'd give for one of those." Later he exclaims, "Hey! There goes a Porsche 944." And jokingly adds, "How about getting me one of those for my birthday?" Still later another car excites him. That father never prepared a lesson entitled, "The Value of Owning an Expensive Sports Car," but his frequent comments taught that lesson clearly.

Modeling is a subtle, "back door" form of communication which is seldom sent or received consciously. While journeying among foreigners, Abraham introduced his wife as his sister. He was afraid that they would kill him to claim his beautiful wife. Isaac, Abraham's son, used the same ploy when he traveled. How was the deceit passed on? Certainly not during a father-son chat. It was simply absorbed through observation.

Modeling is unavoidable — it is not *whether* a person models, but *what* he models. "Every good tree bears good fruit, but a bad tree bears bad fruit" (Matthew 7:17). Dads, most of you are concerned about your children's sexual purity. But are you equally concerned about your purity? What literature do you read? Do you ogle at shapely women? What movies do you rent from the video store? Do you flirt with women other than your wife? What television programs do you watch? Dads must be a portrait of the person they want their children to become.

Secondly, values are transmitted through a person's enthusiasms. When the Apostle Paul wrote to the Thessalonians he said, "Now we really live, since you are standing firm in the Lord" (1 Thessalonians 3:8). What makes you "really live?" Do you become animated when you go shopping, when you attend a basketball game, when you anticipate a round of golf, when you plan an evening of dining? The point is not that you should be grumpy when you go out to eat. But whatever you are *most* passionate about is what your kids will treasure. They unconsciously reason, "If this brings joy to Mom and Dad, it must be worth pursuing."

Recently I was invited to speak in another city. When I returned, I had lunch with a young Christian friend who politely asked how my message had been received. Toward the end of our conversation, I mentioned that I had hunted pheasants on the way home and experienced unusual success. Suddenly, my friend perked up. "You did? Tell me about it. Where did you get them? Did you see very many? Were they difficult shots?" This young man's exuberance unveiled his treasure. Fathers, if you are more enthused by a Don Mattingly home run than the maturing faith of a friend, then your kids will conclude that sports success is supremely important. Moms, if you are more lively about the clothes you bought on sale than your Bible study, your kids will devote themselves to material values.

Compelling images tug at children's hearts — sports heroes, rock and film stars, politicians, the wealthy. If parents want their children's hearts to be captured for God's kingdom, then they must model a vision of serving Him. Unfortunately, many have settled for far less:

As a child, one wants grand things: palaces, kingdoms, flight. Adults settle for a promotion, a house with an extra bathroom, the chair of a committee, an affair with an insurance salesman. All because they have ceased to believe in anything so grand as a destiny, a thing more eternal than stars, more final than death.[2]

And the problem home is not confined to "the unhappy, broken homes . . . , but also the relatively happy ones, where husband and wife like each other and care about their children, very often unselfishly devoting the best parts of their lives to them." Their deficiency is that "they have nothing to give their children in the way of a vision of the world."[3]

Parents, do you want your kids to devote themselves to serving God? Then you must passionately pursue "His kingdom and His righteousness" (see Matthew 6:33). If you are dedicated to ministering to those in prison, or to upholding families with young children, or to sheltering the homeless, or to nurturing a college-age Bible study, it is likely that your children will also adopt eternal values.

Teaching

Isaac committed an immense blunder in training his favorite son, Esau. Though he transmitted his love for the outdoors, he never conveyed the importance of choosing a godly wife. As a result, Esau's choice of Canaanite wives dismayed his parents: "Then Rebekah said to Isaac, 'I'm disgusted with living because of these Hittite women. If Jacob takes a wife from among the women of this land . . . my life will not be worth living' " (Genesis 27:46).

When Esau learned of his parents' disapproval, he desperately sought to amend his error by marrying a wife from the line of Abraham's other son, Ishmael. How tragic! Like all children, Esau wanted to please his parents. But the information came too late. Modeling truth will never be sufficient. It must also be spoken.

Content. Two categories of truth should dominate our instruction. Psalm 78 instructs parents to declare to their offspring "the praiseworthy deeds of the LORD, his power, and the wonders he has done" (v. 4). In addition, they are commanded to inform their children of God's laws and statutes. If one generation is faithful in declaring the *deeds* and the *demands* of the Lord, "then [the next generation will] put their trust in God" (v. 7).

Similarly, Moses advised parents that a call to obedience should be preceded by a reminder of God's "signs and wonders":

Tell [your child]: "We were slaves of Pharaoh in Egypt, but the LORD brought us out of Egypt with a mighty hand. Before our eyes the LORD sent miraculous signs and wonders — great and terrible — upon Egypt and Pharaoh and his whole household. . . . The LORD commanded us to obey all these decrees and to fear the LORD our God, so that we might always prosper and be kept alive, as is the case today." (Deuteronomy 6:21–24)

If parents fail to communicate God's deeds, their kids are barred from knowing the God who makes demands on their conduct at school, at home, at play.

Scripture is the primary source for illuminating the majestic acts of God.

> Who has measured the waters in the hollow of his hand,
>   or with the breadth of his hand marked off the heavens?
> Who has held the dust of the earth in a basket,
>   or weighed the mountains on the scales
>   and the hills in a balance? . . .
> He brings princes to naught
>   and reduces the rulers of this world to nothing.
> No sooner are they planted,
>   no sooner are they sown,
>   no sooner do they take root in the ground,
>   than he blows on them and they wither,

> and a whirlwind sweeps them away like chaff.
>
> (Isaiah 40:12, 23–24)

This God, who knows the weight of the Rocky Mountains, who topples world leaders with a sigh, who fashioned and upholds an infinite universe, is also the God

> [Who] tends his flock like a shepherd:
> He gathers the lambs in his arms
>   and carries them close to his heart;
> He gently leads those that have young.
>
> (Isaiah 40:11)

But God's Word should not be the only testimony to His greatness. Increase Mather's father, Richard, "like many of his contemporaries, had kept a diary and written his autobiography to serve as a guide for his children. Such spiritual autobiographies were an important means of passing values and expectations on from one generation to the next."[4] Similarly, soon after Cathy and I were married, we began recording God's work in our lives. This cumulative journal of God's grace reads like a missionary biography—only it happened to us! These testimonies, periodically reviewed, help sustain the faith of us and our children.

Format. Jesus was an unconventional teacher—no formal classrooms or meeting times; no required books or syllabi. His mobile academy toured funerals, weddings, and parties. His teaching aids were flowers, birds, and trees.

Parents like Jesus are called to communicate truth *informally* in the midst of their children's routines. "Talk about [God's Word] when you sit at home and when you walk along the road, when you lie down and when you get up" (Deuteronomy 6:7).

But to teach informally, parents must adopt a Biblical view of time. The Bible uses two primary words for time: *chronos* and *kairos*. *Chronos* is calendar time. It emphasizes the measurement of time. The other, *kairos*, points toward special moments or happenings. It is time as opportunity. Thus, when Ephesians 5:16 instructs Christians to make the most of the time (*kairos*), they are to make "the most of every opportunity."

Chronological time may intrude into event time. While attending the funeral of my great-aunt, the alarm on someone's watch was triggered. It kept beeping and beeping. Didn't they know how to shut it off? Was it deep in a purse? Was it on the dead body? A funeral is an event which shouldn't be interrupted by the clock. It was a time to grieve, a time to remember, a time to reflect. The time was not 10:35.

Some parents "talk of giving [their] children only quality time . . . , as though human life could be dehydrated and concentrated to avoid the dull spots."[5] But event-time cannot be manufactured. On a cold, blustery afternoon, Cathy was working in the backyard when she heard a child sobbing. She hustled to the front yard to find an agonized, six-year-old girl dragging herself home from school. The distraught girl was making little progress. The burdens of an uncinched backpack, a biting north wind, and her grief were weighing her down. When Cathy tried to comfort her, she poured out her tale of woe. "I wost (lost) my mitten, and I'm going to be wate (late) and my babysitta (babysitter) is going to be woowied (worried)." Cathy assured the little girl that she would search for the mitten and, if found, bring it to her home. My wife then hoisted the backpack onto the girl's back. The sobs were exchanged for a smile and the youngster skipped off to her babysitter. That was a *kairos*, an event that could not have been scheduled in a Day Planner. It occurred only because Cathy was available.

These unplanned incidents are vehicles for relaying God's truth. One evening I was watching the program "Family Ties" with our teenage son, Nathan. Eighteen-year-old Mallory decided to elope with her boyfriend, Nick, to get away from the teasing of her siblings and the nagging of her parents. The next thirty minutes turned out to be a choice occasion to talk with Nathan about marriage:

- Do you think Mallory had an accurate view of marriage?

- Why do you think Mallory is attracted to Nick? What qualities would you look for in a marriage partner?

- Were Mallory and Nick prepared for marriage? What can a couple do to prepare for marriage?

- How would you handle a disagreement with us about a possible marriage partner?

Opportunities to convey truth must be grasped before they evaporate:

The minor Greek god KAIROS was represented by the statue of a young man with wings on his feet and a tuft of hair on the top of his forehead. The word KAIROS means "time," or "opportunity," and these sculptured features give us some idea of how the Greeks viewed the passing of time. The wings indicated that opportunity passes swiftly. Time, as the opportune or fitting moment, is fleeting. The exaggerated forelock implied the need for decisions, for seizing the occasion. Before the moment passes by, we must grab it by the hair. It is this picture of the Greek idea of time which prompted Fredo to comment, "Opportunity may have hair in front, but he is bald in back."[6]

How many parents will awaken to find themselves trying to seize the back of a bald head? If they don't give themselves generously to their young children, the kids may reject their interest in later years. There is still time (chronos) — but there is no time (kairos). As Plato said, "Can there be any doubt that a work is spoiled when it is not done at the right time?"

Since quality time is a residue of quantities of time, parents must squash the idea that "doin' nuthin' " with their kids is a waste of time. Lying down with a child for fifteen minutes at bedtime, lingering at the dinner table, walking the dog are the seeds of those unplannable, special moments.

But an informal style of teaching is not sufficient. We must also teach truth *formally*.

Cathy and I have often been exasperated by our boys' behavior during family worship. They wrangle over the seating arrangement; they yawn; they jump up to go to the bathroom; they stare at the ceiling; they complain about the "excessive" time commitment. But as we have gained an understanding of children, particularly young children, our frustration has been eased.

Babies' first food is milk, followed by cereal, then mashed fruits and vegetables, eventually ground meats. Furthermore, their volume of food is far less than an adult's (though they gobble food during the teen years as if trying to bridge the gap!)

A spiritual diet is similar—"like newborn babies, crave pure spiritual milk, so that by it you may grow up in your salvation" (1 Peter 2:2). What we feed young kids must be monitored because "too many Bible facts and 'advanced' concepts will likely lead to confusion and distortion."[7] Children should *not* attend every church function—more is not necessarily better. Frequently, the children of godly parents show little interest in spiritual matters. We may be gorging them on indigestible food.

When kids reach their early teens (it varies greatly with the individual), they are ready for a meatier diet. External changes—greatly expanded height and weight—coincide with internal changes—new ways of thinking and learning. But even so, their interest in and capability of handling truth blossoms gradually. Our fourteen-year-old studies the Bible twice a week. He and I discuss it once a week. I help him unearth important concepts, explain what he doesn't understand, direct his prayer requests.

Our teaching must not only be digestible but also applicable if we hope to arouse kids' interest. God's Word must shed light on their struggles—pressure to conform to their peers;

the difficulty of loving a younger brother; the problem of being ridiculed for an immature body; the need for a bike.

Furthermore, we can encourage their participation by surrounding family worship with other family fun — playing games together, watching a rented movie, going for a long bicycle ride, or cooking special food.

Finally, our materials will have a bearing on our children's attentiveness. While our boys were young, we used a Bible story book and supplemented it with Scripture. We have also used the guides published by Walk Thru the Bible Ministries. There are a wealth of resources. Experiment to find the one that suits your family.

Accountability. Parents are stewards of children. God is a child's eternal parent and the One he must ultimately please — "We must *all* appear before the judgment seat of Christ, that each one may receive what is due him" (2 Corinthians 5:10, emphasis added). When a child's good work is unappreciated, Dad can remind him that God knows his effort and will commend him for it. When a parent senses that one of his children is lying, he can remind him that he may be able to fool him, but never his Father who "sees in secret." (Now our boys scold each other with "God knows," when they surmise one of their brothers is being dishonest!)

Releasing kids to the Lord also means they increasingly make their own choices. Recently our fourteen-year-old was under pressure to gamble with his friends. In the past, gambling has been off-limits. But we decided to let Nathan make his own decision — though I shared that gambling can strain friendships and involves questionable stewardship. But we told him we would not legislate his behavior; it was between him and Jesus. Our children need a growing realization that their behavior will be judged with eternal consequences.

The Challenge

Children don't dash, run, or even walk into maturity—they creep! God's answer for these plodders is to encompass them with the truth—"Tie [God's commandments] as symbols on your hands and bind them on your foreheads. Write them on the doorframes of your houses and on your gates" (Deuteronomy 6:8–9). One warning to a toddler to stay out of mom's plants will probably not be enough. Nor will one or two discussions with your teens about sex, dating, or money be adequate. Kids' need for repetition can be frustrating—"If I have told you once, I have told you a thousand times!" (In fact, Cathy and I have been tempted to establish a library of taped instructions—"Go listen to Tape #241: Keeping Your Room Clean!") But the nature of growing up demands continual reminders—"impress them . . . talk about them . . . tie them . . . write them . . ."

As mentioned, children's faith cannot be fed with a few, "quality" morsels.

> I often envision this scenario: I as a busy, productive person come to my younger daughter, Kristen, and say, "I cannot talk to you today, dear, but tomorrow at precisely eight o'clock we will have our 'quality time.' Then in the ten minutes allotted you can tell me all your hurts, I will answer all your questions about life, and we will be close."[8]

Parents, it will require lavish portions of time to immerse your kids with the truth.

Moms, must you work full-time? Do you need to work at all? If you are gone all day, who will surround your children with the truth?

What about you, Dads? Moses' instructions were written to you as well. The model in Proverbs is a father teaching his son. Paul singled out fathers for responsibility in nurturing their children's faith. He also assumed that fathers nurtured their children: "You know that we dealt with each of you *as a father deals with his own children, encouraging, comforting and urging* you to live lives worthy of God" (1 Thessalonians 2:11–12, emphasis added). Does that describe the way you relate to your children? Fathers, your children will never adopt your values unless they know you intimately.

> I still have all the benefits of life with a man to whom I was no puzzle to be pieced together and who was no stranger to me. I knew the sinews of his life. I have chosen freely and frequently from what that man let me see of him living his life, and they are the themes of enduring power in my own.[9]

The answer to the time crunch is not time management; it is a clear discernment of God's will. Can it be any clearer, parents, that you are called to surround your children with the truth? Each of you must ask God how you can structure your lives so that you can accomplish that task.

The Role of the Body

God's Word is clear—exposure to a variety of Christians is the foundation for a mature faith. Paul explained: "From [Christ] the whole body, joined and held together by every supporting ligament, grows and builds itself up in love, as each part does its work" (Ephesians 4:15–16). Individual Christian families need the support of "every supporting ligament" in training people to follow the Lord.

Grandparents

Moses instructed parents: "Teach [God's laws] to your children and to their children after them" (Deuteronomy 4:9). Grandparents have been called to transmit their faith to their grandchildren.

During the research for a book on grandparents, a boy was asked to draw a picture of his deceased grandmother. He explained his creation:

> She's saying "How are you, Charles? I hope that you are being a good boy." She's wondering if I still have the ten silver dollars. When I was born she bought ten silver dollars for me to keep and it was a special thing between us. When I look at them I think about her. . . . She said that we can count them in heaven someday. She said that she was sure to go to heaven because she ran her life so she would go there and I should do the same so that we can meet again and be together. Wouldn't that be something?[10]

That boy will probably be in heaven someday because of the magnetic life of his grandmother.

As mentioned, today's grandparents have numerous advantages over their earlier counterparts. They live longer and retire earlier. They have fewer grandkids. They are financially secure. But these gains have seldom translated into deeper relations with their grandchildren. If parents hope to pass the faith onto their children, they must consider how to connect kids with their grandparents.

The Church

The age-segregation of most church activities is a serious hindrance to the transmission of the faith because we are to depend on the *whole* body to develop maturity. Therefore, we must scrutinize the divisions by age, marital status, or stage of family development.

A frequent theme of this book is that kids need a variety of adult models to prepare them for adult life. Unfortunately, most churches feel that a host of youth activities (minus parents) is the way to minister to the young. But youth leaders, who are often recent converts, are too few and too undeveloped to nurture full Christian maturity in kids.

Age mixing is important for adults as well. I lean on others to prepare me for untrod paths — parents who have successfully raised teenagers, men who have gone through a mid-life crisis, Christians negotiating retirement. Additionally, by staying in touch with new parents, single adults, widows, and the divorced, I remain sensitive to their needs.

So how can the church reunite the generations? Sunday school classes of contrasting ages can be joined for two or three months each year. Family camps can be stressed instead of age-restrictive ones. Teenagers can be included in adult Bible studies. Special intergenerational worship can be scheduled (e.g., a New Year's Eve service to jointly share the blessings of the past year). Adults can mentor individual teens or an entire youth Sunday school class.

In addition, parents, you can increase your kids' contact with adults by housing visiting missionaries, by sharing family worship with another family, by inviting mature Christians to share a meal, by including a single adult, a grandparent, or another family on your vacations.

Conclusion

God's Word is clear — a healthy body has all the ligaments and sinews working in concert. The faith of our children will be stunted if we depend only on individual families to pass on the faith.

PART FIVE

PHYSICAL TRAINING

13

LEISURE IN THE HOME

Better one handful with tranquility
than two handfuls with toil
and chasing after the wind.

(Ecclesiastes 4:6)

T ime has become so precious that we double up activities to conserve time:

- We read the paper while we converse with our mates.

- We listen to motivational tapes while we jog.

- We study while we watch T.V.

- We run errands while we spend time with our kids.

- We wash the dishes while we talk on the phone.

- We plan the coming week during Sunday morning worship.

- We read a magazine while we move our bowels.

Even our leisure is not leisurely. Our recreation is sandwiched between tight schedules. Our meals are gulped. A free evening is as rare as a whooping crane.

But what is leisure? How should it be practiced in the home? Light can be shed on those questions by a brief historical view of leisure.

Historical Perspective

The Meaning of Leisure

"What do you do?"

"I am a husband."

"Well, of course," he chuckled, "but what do you really do?"

"I am also a father, a son, and a neighbor."

"I mean," he said nervously, "what is your vocation?"

"I think my primary calling in life is to serve my seventh grade boys' Sunday school class and their families."

"You get paid to do that?!"

"Oh, no. It is a voluntary service."

"I don't think you understand what I was asking. What do you do to earn a living?"

"Oh, that. I run a janitorial service."

The ancient Greeks would not have been baffled by this man's answers. Unlike us, they did not define people by their work. Can you imagine the Apostle Paul answering the question, "What do you do?" with "I'm a tentmaker"?

It was leisure, rather than work, that was dominant for the Greeks. However, before picturing a toga-clad Greek hunking down in front of the T.V. with a six-pack of beer, we must understand the Greek definition of leisure. The Greek word for leisure is *schole*. From this word come "the English words school and scholarship. Leisure, then, was a time for growth and development."[1] Reading, thinking, studying, and conversing were the free man's primary forms of leisure. It wasn't peripheral; it was central. It wasn't something that revived people for work, it was creative, fulfilling in itself.

The Amount of Leisure

Most periods of history allotted *more* time for leisure than we do today:

> From Classical Antiquity, the number of holidays or 'holy days' was around 115 a year. Although some people in those times worked long hours, this was true only during certain periods in the year. Winter months were less hectic and, as in certain trades today, inclement weather often provided a welcome respite from labor. Most urban citizens worked a short day.[2]

Theoretically, a forty-hour job leaves ample time for leisure. But commuting, moonlighting, and overtime may devour that time.

Furthermore, daily rhythms were traditionally more relaxed — an attitude still reflected in some cultures:

> In the middle of the day, in the heat of the sun, in many if not most parts of the agrarian world, labor ceases, shelter is sought, food and people come together, time out is called, to eat and digest.[3]

But today an "office or factory worker would need a certificate from a physician to take a rest or a nap after lunch."[4]

The Context of Leisure

My three boys play on separate soccer teams. With a fifteen-game schedule and about one practice for each game, they each have about thirty activities twice yearly (there are fall and spring seasons). These 180 activities — which are mindboggling to squeeze into our schedule — tear at family togetherness. But the context for leisure in traditional society was the family, not the peer group. Games were played at home. Parties were family affairs — not until the nineteenth century did parents plan parties exclusively for children. The entire family entertained guests.

Furthermore, leisure was wrapped in a social setting. Visiting neighbors, sitting on the porch, stopping at a café before work, attending a community dance were excuses to commune. But today, we attend an aerobics class to exercise, we play racquetball for the competitive challenge, and we attend a movie to be entertained. We don't even have time for casual conversation afterward. We have to pick up the kids, get to the dentist, or rush home to fix dinner.

The Downfall of Leisure

The erosion of leisure began when Americans became fearful of squandering time. A nineteenth-century student warned:

> The men the boys will become, will sit in the Bar room while their families are left in dark cellars to starve. Think of it. Thousands have perished in this way. I warn you to guard against this evil. . . . For remember "time flies on Eagle's wings," and if you lose it once, you can never catch it again. A great many have written on this subject, but I do not think too much can be said about so great a sin as Idleness.[5]

Prodded on by the common wisdom of the day—the McGuffey readers declared: "One doer is worth a hundred dreamers."—Americans rushed into a frenzy of activity.

Initially, only men became hostages to time. Most moms and children lived a freer life. But equality has come—everyone lives a harried life! I recently heard of a working mother who dresses her children at bedtime to conserve time in the morning rush.

Biblical Guidelines

Loving God and Neighbor

The Bible says little about leisure—but it speaks loudly about our primary callings in life: "Love the Lord your God with all your heart and with all your soul and with all your mind and with all your strength. . . . Love your neighbor as yourself" (Mark 12:30–31). Therefore, activities that build our love for God and people should fill our leisure.

Unfortunately, most of our leisure is escapist — a round of golf or an outing at an amusement park or watching T.V. Such activities offer a respite from life's hassles but do little to fortify our spirits. What kind of leisure, then, will build a love for God? Reading God's Word or a good book, recording God's blessings in a journal, walking in a park, listening to uplifting music, praying alone or with a friend, joining a weekly Bible study, or attending a retreat.

And what kind of leisure will enable us to serve people? Inviting a friend to lunch, arranging a date with your spouse, repairing a friend's car, fixing a special meal for guests, visiting prisoners, growing vegetables to share with others, and much, much more.

But enjoying productive leisure does not mean that we must pack our non-work hours with "enriching" activities. The church Fathers spoke of a "holy leisure" which:

> refers to a sense of balance in the life, an ability to be at peace through the activities of the day, an ability to rest and take time to enjoy beauty, an ability to pace ourselves.[6]

Nor will quality leisure exclude all golf or Sunday afternoon football games. But it may effect the frequency or the form of those activities. If we plan to watch a football game, we could make it a social affair by including others.

Working Wholeheartedly

Paul reminded the Thessalonians that he labored night and day to serve them. He instructed the Colossians to work with all their hearts. Do these statements endorse a frantic workaholism? By no means. First of all, the Thessalonians were famous for their idleness. Paul would have delivered a different message to those who overwork — as Jesus did to Martha.

Furthermore, when Paul urged the Colossians to be devoted to their work, he also told them to be devoted to prayer (see Colossians 4:2). Elsewhere, he told Christians to be devoted to one another (see Romans 12:10) and devoted to good deeds (see Titus 3:14). Therefore, when Paul instructs us to work wholeheartedly, he is not asking us to work incessantly or to ignore other commitments. Neither is he endorsing the sixty-hour work week nor a yearly cycle of fifty weeks on the job and two weeks of vacation. He is simply telling us to work diligently when we labor.

Sometimes I act as if the headless horseman is driving me to my writing. I try to participate in family life, but I am preoccupied with the disarray in a chapter or struggling to find a unique word for a heading. Recently, I asked Cathy to guide the kids toward bed because I wanted to write. But as coincidences happen, I was working on this section. As I reflected, I was convicted that I had not recently spent time with my eldest. I reluctantly pulled myself from the computer. The conversation drifted into a discussion of what qualities to look for in a mate. Who knows — those few minutes could save him and us a lifetime of grief from marrying unwisely. The twenty to thirty minutes I spend many nights reading, talking, and praying with my boys is crucial for their development.

Enjoying God's Gifts

Our culture has been warped by the concept — first posited by economist Adam Smith — that an act is useful only if it produces something. One truth, "subdue the earth," has been distorted by making it man's only vocation.

Under Smith's definition of productivity, making love with your spouse, enjoying a dinner out, marveling at a sunset, or taking a vacation would be "unproductive."

But God intends for us to enjoy His gifts:

[W]hen God gives any man wealth and possessions, and enables him to enjoy them, . . . this is a gift of God. (Ecclesiastes 5:19)

Enjoy life with your wife, whom you love. (Ecclesiastes 9:9)

[False teachers] forbid people to marry and order them to abstain from certain foods, which God created to be received with thanksgiving. . . . For everything God created is good, and nothing is to be rejected if it is received with thanksgiving. (1 Timothy 4:3–4)

Command those who are rich in this present world not to be arrogant nor to put their hope in wealth, which is so uncertain, but to put their hope in God, *who richly provides us with everything for our enjoyment.* (1 Timothy 6:17, emphasis added)

Though now I know better, my psyche is still hung over from an addiction to the productivity gospel. I feel anxious when a conversation with my elderly neighbor lingers. I frequently want to return early from a vacation. I find it difficult to postpone my writing to write a letter to a friend. I feel guilty if I ride bikes with my kids on a weekday afternoon.

Conclusion

Biblical leisure should challenge, move, renew, calm, educate, and strengthen God's people. Unfortunately, most of our leisure leaves us hyped, exhausted, or dulled. We must reshape the practice of our leisure to fulfill our highest callings: to love God and His people.

Practical Principles

Slowing Down

A missionary friend serving on an island in the Caribbean found it difficult to adjust to the sluggish pace of the islanders. They were seldom on time. Once they arrived, they stayed forever. On one occasion, he went to the port city to check on the arrival of parts for his ailing Jeep. The customs official informed him that his package had not arrived. When the official saw my friend's frustration, he asked, "Why are you so upset? It will probably be on the boat next month."

"Next month!" Our focus is on minutes and seconds. Football games kickoff at 5:12. We apologize profusely if we are five minutes late for an appointment. We tune our pastors out when the clock strikes 12:01.

But God encourages us to walk, not run, through life. The prophet Isaiah proclaimed, "in repentance and rest is your salvation, in quietness and trust is your strength" (Isaiah 30:15). The spiritual life cannot be nurtured in allegro.

> I wasted an hour one morning
>   beside a mountain stream,
> I seized a cloud from the sky above
>   and fashioned myself a dream,
> In the hush of the early twilight,
>   far from the haunts of men,
> I wasted a summer evening,
>   and fashioned my dream again.
> Wasted? Perhaps.
>   Folks say so who never have walked with God,
> When lanes are purple with lilacs
>   or yellow with goldenrod.
> But I have found strength for my labors
>   in that one short evening hour.
> I have found joy and contentment;
>   I have found peace and power.
> My dreaming has left me a treasure,
>   a hope that is strong and true.
> From wasted hours I have built my life
>   and found my faith anew.[7]

It is in reading and thinking and praying and listening that we come to know God. Spiritual food cannot be gulped between other activities.

God also desires a more relaxed tempo in human relationships. A newly wed Israelite was freed from work and military duties for one year so that he could "bring happiness" to his bride (see Deuteronomy 24:5). Wow! A year-long honeymoon! A marriage is built on chunks of time, uninterrupted by kids or work or telephones or housework.

Hectic lifestyles begin in childhood. "We have kept our children so busy with 'useful' and 'improving' activities, that we are in danger of raising a generation of young people who are terrified of silence, of being alone with their own thoughts."[8]

If we want our kids to be friends with silence, we must protect them from busyness. With our boys, we don't allow them to participate in more than one sport at a time. When summer comes, we don't let them play with friends from sunup to sundown. They have daily (forty-five minutes each afternoon), weekly (Sunday is a family day), and seasonal (three to four weeks a year of family vacation) periods of rest.

Balancing Work and Leisure

The American pattern of work has left little time for leisure until retirement at sixty to sixty-five. We work forty plus hours a week, forty-eight to fifty weeks a year, thirty to forty years.

But the Biblical pattern blends work and leisure. Following Paul's conversion, he argued in the synagogues that Jesus was the Messiah. This flurry of activity was followed by three years of solitude in Arabia. Then,

> despite his call to take the gospel to the Gentiles, he spent the next eleven years in Cilicia, his home region (Galatians 1:21). Following a spell in Antioch (Acts 11:25f), his call was renewed and he began the first of his great missionary journeys (Acts 13:1ff). . . . Sometimes he moved on rapidly

from one place to the next. At other times he settled down
for two or three years in the one city. At various points
where he was imprisoned, he was forced to withdraw from
his journeyings.[9]

But, like Paul, do we have to be shackled to slow down?
Hopefully not! Each summer our family pares its commitments for about six weeks. I take a break from teaching and
speaking. We limit the kids athletics. We mow less because
the summer heat stunts the grass. The garden is planted,
weeded, growing; we only water and harvest. Our evenings
are reserved for relaxed fellowship—bike rides, visits with
friends, book reading.

There are other ways to free chunks of time—part-time
work rather than full-time; an arrangement with your employer for six to eight weeks of vacation each year (even
though some may be without pay); job sharing; or taking an
extended break when you change jobs. Plan carefully. Time is
to be used wisely, not hectically.

Many wives report that their husbands have a difficult time
unwinding—even on vacations. However, it may take more
than a week of vacation to calm our minds and our hearts.

Discerning God's Will

"Only lazy people work hard." What? It sounds like saying, "Tall people are short." Pastor Eugene Peterson explains
that they are *lazy* because they avoid the difficult process of
"deciding and directing, establishing values and setting
goals."[10] And they *work hard* because aimless people often become enslaved to others.

We find ourselves frantically, at the last minute, trying to
satisfy a half dozen different demands on our time, none of
which is essential to our vocation, to stave off the disaster
of disappointing someone.[11]

Many pastors wear the word "busy" as a badge of honor. Peterson believes otherwise:

> The word *busy* is the symptom not of commitment, but of betrayal. It is not devotion but defection. The adjective *busy* set as a modifier to *pastor* should sound to our ears like *adulterous* to characterize a wife, or *embezzling* to describe a banker. It is an outrageous scandal, a blasphemous affront.[12]

It is a scandal because he has confused the demands of people with the demands of God.

People will press us to succumb to their will. They may appeal to our egos — "No one can do the job like you can." Or they may stir our guilt — "Listen, if you don't do it, the job just won't get done." Or they may invoke a purported divine authority: "This is God's work. He has called us to complete this task and you are a part of it." Or they may simply wear us down with persistence. However, if we let others control our lives, we will burn up our lives "tending urgent little brush fires."[13]

When I am controlled by the agendas of others, family commitments suffer. No one begs me to tuck my boys in each night. No one pleads with me to vacation with my wife. No one exhorts me to teach the Scriptures to my sons. Yet such tasks are God's will for me.

Jesus did not walk through every open door. The morning after ministering in Capernaum, He found a solitary place to pray (see Mark 1:35–38). When His friends found Him, they exclaimed: "Everyone is looking for You!" What an opportunity! The crowds were eager for Jesus. But Jesus told His disciples: "Let us go somewhere else — to the nearby villages — so that I can preach there also. *That is why I have come.*" Jesus knew why He had come. He understood that opportunity and the Father's will may not coincide.

A friend inherited a family business that was in shambles from years of neglect. In trying to clean up the mess, he found himself working sixty- to seventy-hour weeks, but still not completing his work. As he was confronted with God's calling on his *whole* life, he made an immediate adjustment — he cut down to ten-hour days and refused to work weekends. Some time later he told me that he still wasn't finishing his work. But he was unconcerned, enjoying the freedom that comes from obedience.

Rejecting Materialism

Materialism forces us to work more. A larger home not only increases our house payments, but also our taxes, utility bills, outlays for furnishings, and repair bills. And we work overtime, add a part-time job, or send mom to work to fund these extras.

Furthermore, even if we have unlimited resources, our possessions can still trample leisure:

> All these damned machines and gadgets, all the things I bought thinking they would serve me well; they suck the life right out of me, an hour at a time. Traipsing back and forth to repair shops, I see precious chunks of life being paid out as ransom for my addiction to consumer goods. . . . Every purchase I make, and the inevitable time it will eventually cost in care and feeding, serves mainly to divert me from the genuine joys of living — being with my family and other friends, writing, sailing, building, daydreaming.[14]

Solomon, one of the wealthiest men of all time, understood that there is freedom in simplicity:

> The sleep of a laborer is sweet, whether he eats little or much, but the abundance of a rich man permits him no sleep. (Ecclesiastes 5:12)

Choosing Quality

Entertainment—T.V., sporting events, amusement parks, movies—dominates our leisure. Such activities are like "cotton candy to the soul"; they are okay as a frivolous treat but should never become a staple of our diets.

As mentioned, quality leisure builds people—evening-long conversations, prayer and Bible study, playing a musical instrument, a walk along a creek, gardening, visiting a patient in a retirement home, cooking, writing, sewing, painting, furniture repair, and so much more.

But we can't do it all. Formerly, I felt deficient when I saw a man repairing his car—knowing my auto skills are limited to being able to pump my own gas. However, if you garden and visit prisoners, you aren't also compelled to play a musical instrument and make all your own Christmas presents and serve as a deacon in your church. Our gifts, interests, and opportunities will cause our leisure to vary.

Furthermore, quality leisure blends the generations. As has been stressed, kids are adrift without adult guidance. We must plan leisure that reunites the ages—family potluck dinners, an entire family preparing a meal for a sick family, an outing at the lake with teens and their families, or a mixed-age Bible study.

Vacationing

We need vacations from our vacations. We race around the country, visiting a "chocolate box assortment of sites" and return home exhausted. One family found that spending a month each summer on an island retreat was more satisfying: "With no bridges, no roads, and no commercial ferry access to this place, the water is a friendly moat. It holds in abeyance the tide of busyness which surges against us the rest of the year."[15]

Vacations can also be a time for service. Recently, I overheard a conversation between two recruiters for a church's vacation Bible school. One of their recruits offered to give up a week of her vacation to teach—but one of the organizers was horrified at the thought. But why? I have friends who have traveled to distant lands to build churches, to give medical care, and to relieve missionaries; others volunteer a week of their vacation to serve at a church camp; others use vacation time to help with church repairs. Our vacations should focus on God's vision of leisure—not our travel agent's.

Conclusion

Karen Wise's friend frequently promised that when her schedule eased, she would invite Karen for a visit. But it never happened.

> I've decided that either she doesn't want to get together at all, or she's waiting for a domestic miracle. She's probably looking for the clear day on her calendar that coincides with the same time the kids are at Grandmother's, and the maid just happens to leave two fruit cups, two cheese Danish, and two cups of hot tea sitting on the counter.

Leisure must be planned. A date with your wife, coffee with a friend, a day of study and planning, or an outing with your daughter must be placed in your date book and guarded closely.

Your appointment calendar is a gift. When you schedule an evening with your daughter, you can refuse a request to help paint the church that same night. If you are timid, you can merely say, "I'm sorry, I already have something planned." But if you want to be an apostle for Biblical leisure, you can say, "I'm sorry I can't help paint that night because I have a date with my daughter." Why are we sheepish about family commitments?

Saying "no" to the good so that you can say "yes" to the best is difficult. Eliot Daley mourned the good things that needed pruning:

I simply must terminate fully half of what I am doing, and that makes me sorry. And grumpy. I am facing for the first time the serious realization that I cannot do all I dream of doing.[16]

Parents, you cannot do everything. But you can do everything your heavenly Father calls you to do.

14

FAMILY HEALTH

*If normal food habits . . . were fully understood and practiced, .
. . disease would practically disappear, crime would subside, in-
sanity would be scarcely if at all in evidence, and there would
be less, very much less, imbecility and physical and mental imperfection in our wonderful country.*

W. H. Hay, 1934[1]

The conflicting advice from health specialists can be dizzying:

- Some nutritionists believe breakfast should be our largest meal, citing evidence that a skimpy breakfast has a negative effect in the workplace. But others advocate only fruit and fruit juices before noon.

- One expert warns that drinking water with a meal will dilute our digestive juices. Another counsels that meals "should always include an adequate supply of liquid."

- The American Academy of Pediatrics concludes that there is no absolute reason to circumcise newborns.

But another reputable source tells us: "You won't be making a mistake" if you circumcise your infant son.

- One health advisor contends that mixing proteins and carbohydrates at the same meal, "retards and even prevents digestion." Another authority counters: "There is no scientific evidence that any one type of food should not be combined with another."

- A decade ago researchers believed that salt contributed to higher blood pressure. But they now suspect that a calcium deficiency has a greater influence.

Why can't "experts" agree? The answer, in part, is that "human chemistry at the cellular level is extremely complex."[2] Thus, trying to find *the* cause for cholesterol-plugged arteries is like trying to find *the* cause for World War II—few processes in life are controlled by a single factor.

Future generations may chuckle at our health "facts" like we chuckle at our ancestors who believed that eating salmon caused leprosy. Therefore, I must administer the following health advice with a large dose of humility.

Family Health

The Scriptures and Sickness

Modern life divorces medical and Biblical truth. We tend to believe that "if you are physically sick you go to the hospital, but if you have a spiritual need you may turn a different corner down a separate lane and go to the church."[3] But God's Word has important insights into the sources and remedies of sickness.

Some afflictions are sent by God to punish sin. Paul informed the Corinthians that many of them were sick, some had even died, because they had profaned the Lord's Supper. He told them the cure was to "examine" themselves—to uncover and confess the offending sins (see 1 Corinthians 11:27–32).

But not all infirmities are a result of sin. When the disciples noticed a blind man, they asked Jesus: "Rabbi, who sinned, this man or his parents, that he was born blind?" Jesus answered: "Neither this man nor his parents sinned, but this happened so that the work of God might be displayed in his life" (John 9:2–3). As we rely on God's grace to overcome our handicaps, we shed light on a world battling similar defects. Joni Erickson Tada's response to quadriplegia has certainly given her a greater ministry than she could have had with a healthy body.

God also sends disease as a form of instruction. Paul explained why God wouldn't heal his infirmity:

> But he said to me, "My grace is sufficient for you, for my power is made perfect in weakness." Therefore, I will boast all the more gladly about my weaknesses, so that Christ's power may rest on me. (2 Corinthians 12:9)

Cathy is allergic to tree pollens in the spring. For about six weeks, her throat is sore, her head pounds, her sinuses are bloated, her nose runs, her energy is nonexistent. Her allergies have been her tutor to teach her how to depend on God's strength. This type of suffering lingers until we graduate into immortality.

Furthermore, physical suffering is also the work of Satan. Jesus encountered a woman who had been crippled by Satan for eighteen years. When our bodies become a battleground of the spirit world, prayer will be the most effective remedy.

Finally, ill health is also a result of mistreating our bodies. If we eat an imbalanced diet or smoke, we may suffer painful consequences. The cure in this case is learning how to take care of our bodies.

A Biblical perspective on sickness is essential. Without it we or our children may:

- feel guilty, believing that all physical problems are due to sin or a lack of faith.

- fail to discern the influence of our spiritual health on our physical health.

- forget that prayer is an important component in overcoming sickness.

- become bitter at a God who does not remove our pain.

Taking Care of Ourselves

We control many factors that influence our health. These include: "personal eating habits, smoking, exercise, and stress; the healthfulness of the air, water and food ingested; and the conditions of the workplace. . . ." Thus, "the greatest potential for improving the health of the American people is probably not to be found in increasing the number of physicians or hospital beds but rather in what people can be motivated to do for themselves."[4]

Similarly, we have great influence over the health of our children:

> The most important elements in the diagnosis of illness are behavior change, appearance, and the medical history of the child. As the parent, you are very sensitive to your child's behavior patterns, quick to note a change in his or her appearance, and totally familiar with the child's medical history, your own, and probably those of your parents as well. The typical pediatrician, whose assembly line spews out thirty, forty, or even fifty patients a day, doesn't know your child as you do and has neither the time nor the inclination to learn.[5]

Nathan battled a rash on his legs and arms for several years. Doctors prescribed special soaps and cremes — which only minimally controlled the problem. One day, Cathy observed that his rashes occurred where his clothing rubbed against his body — collar, sleeves, and tops of socks. She wondered if the irritations were due to laundry detergent. After experimenting, she discovered that Nathan was allergic to bleach; a bleach substitute cured the problem. When Andrew was a toddler, he had recurring diarrhea. Our doctor advised feeding him liquids, but that counsel only made him weak and cranky. While reading a book on nutrition, we learned that food allergies can cause diahrrea (a possibility our doctor had not suggested, which is not surprising since only thirteen percent of a recent group of medical school graduates believed doctors should be knowledgeable about nutrition[6]). We tested the common allergies and found that Andrew was allergic to wheat. When wheat was eliminated from his diet, his stools changed immediately. Observant and instructed parents can diagnose and treat many of their children's illnesses.

The Role of Doctors

Pediatrician Robert Mendelsohn states that the vast majority of visits to the doctor are unnecessary. In fact, he claims ninety-five percent of kids' illnesses will heal themselves and what the doctors are really treating is parental distress!

But, as one doctor observed, "placebo" treatments serve a purpose:

> It's often said that doctors "play God," but the comment misses the point. Whether or not we're trying to be God's understudies, we always play to our audience. The truth is that people expect it of us. . . . In offices, clinics and hospitals, we give performances calculated to make people feel better.[7]

And if the doctor is unwilling to perform, his patient will go home "with serious questions about his health — and [the doctor's] competence."

Mendelsohn's book, *How to Raise a Healthy Child . . . in Spite of Your Doctor*, can relieve parental distress without a visit to a doctor. It dispenses advice on the treatment of common illnesses and the symptoms of serious illness when your child needs medical help.

Avoiding unnecessary treatments may be crucial. "Every year at least three hundred thousand people suffer such severe reactions to drugs prescribed for them by doctors that they are forced to go for treatment to a hospital, eighteen thousand patients who are given drugs while in the (ospital die from the side effects, and some ten thousand people suffer life-threatening reactions from prescribed drugs."[8]

A friend's doctor recommended gall bladder surgery to relieve her abdominal pains. While rechecking her medical charts minutes before surgery, he found that her gall bladder had been removed during an earlier operation. He decided to operate anyway! We must confront our doctors — never an easy task — with questions. If they don't have adequate answers, we should not submit to their treatments.

Exercise

Imagine a nineteenth-century farmer being dropped into a modern fitness center with exercise bikes, weight machines, running tracks, and stationary rowers. At first he would be dazzled by the slick, stainless steel equipment. But the longer he observed the labor of the athletes, the more puzzled he would become: "Do those machines do anything?"

They may not do much — in spite of fitness centers and fancy equipment, eighty percent of Americans are not physically fit. Why? In spite of all the helps, many of us aren't willing to pay the price. Physical fitness is

> still part of an elusive dream — an exercise (or non-exercise, actually) in futility. Finding an exercise that requires minimal time and effort and yet yields a high payoff and a guarantee of a body that is fit and beautiful continues to elude most Americans.[9]

There are no quick fixes. A tuned body requires time and discipline.

Aerobic Exercise

Cardiovascular endurance is the cornerstone to fitness. It is measured by

> the ability of your heart . . . to deliver oxygen to the body's cells. Although muscles can draw on quick sources of energy for short-term exertion, when exercise lasts longer than a minute or two, the muscles get most of their energy from a process that requires oxygen from the blood. Because of the role played by oxygen, such activities are called *aerobic* (meaning "with air").[10]

Regular aerobic workouts of fifteen to sixty minutes a day, three to five days a week will give a person's heart the ability to deliver more oxygen to the body's cells.

The benefits of aerobic exercise. Since we live in a culture committed to the "cult of physical well-being," it is important to remember what exercise will *not* do for you:

- It will not impart eternal life.

- It will not save a dying marriage.

- It will not make your kids obedient.

- It will not balance your checkbook.

As the Apostle Paul stated, physical training has some value, but is not supremely important.

However, aerobic exercise does have considerable value. The benefits include: decreased blood pressure, increased respiration, toned muscles, stronger bones, increased energy, smoother digestion and elimination, decreased fatty deposits in the arteries, and a savings of ten to twenty thousand heartbeats a day.[11] One study found that the *least* active people were almost twice as likely to have heart disease as those who were *most* active.[12] (Less strenuous forms of exercise like yard work or square dancing carry some benefit.)

Furthermore, doctors have found that exercise aids in the healing process. Thus, they rouse hospital patients onto their feet as soon as possible.

Finally, exercise is an effective means of weight control. A two hundred pound person who decides to walk briskly 1.5 miles per day — and whose diet remains unchanged — will lose about fourteen pounds in a year.

Choosing a program. Swimming, bicycling, running, basketball, cross country skiing, walking, racquetball, and handball are among the activities that sufficiently stress the heart. Cathy and I enjoy brisk walking because we encounter few limitations on the time, place, or weather. And we are free to talk or pray with no interfering children or phone calls.

But a weekly stroll isn't worth much. It must be thirty to forty minutes of brisk walking three to five times a week. (A brisk walk is approximately four miles per hour — a rate that beginners should ease into.)

Unfortunately, the benefits of exercise dissolve quickly:

> If you train for six months and then stop, you've done nothing to decrease your long-term chances of developing heart disease. Studies have shown that even Olympic athletes who stop training when their careers are over quickly revert back to having the same risk of heart disease as individuals who never exercised at all.[13]

Thus, in choosing a program we should focus on activities that we can continue into our senior years. No amount of exercise in our twenties or thirties will provide lifelong benefits.

Family Exercise

A whopping twenty-seven percent of six- to eleven-year-olds and twenty-two percent of twelve- to seventeen-year-olds are obese—up fifty percent from the late 1960s.[14] Because aerobic exercise helps control weight, we have steered our kids toward demanding sports like soccer and basketball—rather than softball or volleyball.

Parents, the way you spend time together can draw your kids into exercise. Our family time includes biking around the city, walking to a close-by restaurant, cross country skiing on a Saturday afternoon, swimming at the YMCA. And on vacations, we don't lounge by a pool all day—we hike, swim, paddle canoes.

If your child prefers less strenuous sports like golf or softball, encourage other exercise. We schedule exercise into our home school curriculum. We reward exercise—lately, rope jumping has earned time on Grandma's Nintendo. We help them organize a touch football game. We ask them to bike to the store to get a carton of milk. We make them walk or bike to visit friends. In spite of their complaints that "all the other kids' parents give rides" or "I'm coming down with something" or "it's too cold" or "it's too hot" or "it's too far" or "I won't get there on time"—biking is healthy for them. Our kids even ride their bikes during winter—they just bundle up a bit more.

Most Christians don't smoke, believing it desecrates the body, the temple of the Holy Spirit. But is it less of a desecration to allow arteries to clog and hearts to weaken? If you or your children are too busy to exercise, you are busier than God wants you to be.

Nutrition

People have wrangled over diet for centuries. The Babylonians didn't believe vegetables could sustain Daniel and his friends. During seventeenth-century England, some ate cabbage heartily, while others believed it caused depression. (That rumor was probably started by a child who did not like cabbage!) During that same period, some thought sugar produced "dangerous effects in the body."[15] But others concluded that something which could preserve fruit must have similar capabilities in humans:

> That which preserves Apples and Plums,
> Will also preserve Liver and Lungs.

These early nutritionists were mostly guessing. Today, however, we stand on sounder footings. Science is responsible for finding the cure for nutritional diseases like pellagra and rickets. Science has discovered the components of food (vitamins) and now knows which foods make up a healthy diet. Though some aspects of nutritional science remain controversial, many are generally affirmed.

Imbalanced Diets

American calorie consumption has changed little during this century. But our calories have come increasingly from animal protein — meat and dairy products — and saturated fats. As a result, our intake of fiber has steadily decreased. These dietary changes have frequently been linked with increased heart disease and some forms of cancer.[16]

Leo Tolstoy believed meat eating was "quite unnecessary, and only [served] to develop animal feelings, to excite desire, to promote fornication and drunkenness."[17] Though meat is still derided — but not for immorality! — the primary problem may be the quantities in which it is consumed. Meat is an important source of protein, B vitamins, iron, and zinc.

The best dietary advice for most Americans, then, is to eat more fruits, whole grains, and vegetables. By studying tables of food composition found in books on nutrition, you can pick the more nutritious foods. (e.g. From our studies, we determined to eat more broccoli — one cup delivers ninety percent of RDA of A, two hundred percent of C, eight percent of iron and protein, and twenty-five percent of fiber!)

Nutritional Myths

We Americans are deeply infected with the disease of gullibility. If someone declares: "Research has demonstrated . . . " or "Dr. Knows-A-Lot has discovered that . . . ", we are ready to submit our bodies to the wildest treatments. We must be careful—the health industry has more quacks per square inch than the duck pond at your local zoo. (A reliable health newsletter can help you ferret out the imposters. *Berkeley Wellness Letter*, P.O. Box 10922, Des Moines, IA 50340; or *Nutrition Action Health Letter*, 1501 16th St., N.W., Washington, D.C., 20036)

You may believe the ideas I label "myths" are gospel truth. And you may be right. (I am still waiting for God to engrave the Ten Commandments of Health!) But remember to ask yourself—Why do I believe this? What is the basis for my opinion?

Myth #1: Food processing removes most vitamins from food.

This is a partial myth. Cooking, freezing, and canning do leech nutrients out of food. But a significant amount of food value remains. Compare the effect of various food preparations on the nutrients in summer squash:[18]

Preparation	Vitamin A	Thiamine	Vitamin C
Raw	338 IU	.05 mg	8.4 mg
Fresh, boiled/drained	287	.05	5.5
Frozen, boiled/drained	195	.04	6.8
Canned, boiled/drained	121	.02	2.7

Though fresh or minimally cooked produce is best, processed food still contains significant nutrition.

Myth #2: Calories ingested in the evening are more likely to be stored as fat than food eaten earlier in the day.

But research by Dr. Artemis Simopoulos, director of nutritional sciences at the International Life Sciences Institute Research Foundation, found that when food was eaten had no correlation to fat production.[19]

Myth #3: Massive doses of vitamins can ward off disease.

Claims have been made that massive doses of vitamins can cure certain diseases. Though vitamin supplements can be beneficial, a person must be cautious about ingesting doses far in excess of the recommended daily allowance. Large quantities of vitamins A and D are especially dangerous. These vitamins are stored in the body's fat tissue and can build up to toxic levels.

Myth #4: Cancer is more widespread today because of the increased use of herbicides, pesticides, and food additives.

The cancer rate is increasing. But "if we exclude lung cancer deaths from the death rates, we find that the overall cancer death rates remain fairly constant."[20] Thus, smoking is the primary reason for the rise in the cancer rate.

However, caution is needed because the long-term effects of many chemicals are unknown. "According to the National Academy of Sciences, only about a fifth of all pesticides sold in the United States have been adequately tested for cancer risk, only about half for their role in causing birth defects and only ten percent for adverse effects on the nervous system."[21] Because of these uncertainties, it is wise to grow as many of your own fruits and vegetables as possible and buy your food from producers who use minimal chemicals.

Myth #5: Dairy products should be avoided or greatly reduced.

As the son of a dairyman, I must attack this myth—or endanger my inheritance! Milk fat has been denounced for its role in heart disease. But "milk is an excellent food—an excellent source of calcium (about ¾ of calcium available to Americans comes from milk products), vitamins D and B-12, and quality proteins."[22]

Though it may be advisable to use lowfat dairy products, a diet that excludes milk and cheese may cause serious problems. For example, elderly women with a history of calcium deficiency will likely develop a degenerative bone disease that leaves their bones weak and brittle.

Kids and Nutrition

Children are exasperating. Though you reiterate the basics of nutrition, though you labor to prepare healthy food, and though you seldom buy junk food, they may still prefer Sugar Crisps to granola, a Twinkie to homemade bread, and pop to fruit juice. But hang on — though values are transmitted slowly, they *are* transmitted. Your children will eventually copy most of your values.

In the interim, kids' diets can be improved by providing healthy snacks. We keep our fruit bowl filled. I peel oranges or cut up apples for everyone while we watch T.V. We munch on popcorn rather than candy or cookies. Cathy bakes with nuts, dried fruit, and some whole wheat flour. We halve the sugar in many recipes — now we can taste the natural ingredients! We limit our boys' purchases of sweets.

Furthermore, we encourage a balanced diet by requiring second helpings of meat to be preceded by seconds on vegetables. (This also curbs overeating. A satisfied child might squeeze more barbecued chicken into his stomach — but not chicken and squash.) We also ask them to periodically taste foods they don't like. Andrew had a narrow range of likes as a child. Many meals he ate cottage cheese, fruit, and carrots, while we ate other foods. We did not force him to eat large helpings of foods he didn't like, only to keep trying them. Recently at a Chinese restaurant, he insisted that we order the Deluxe Vegetables.

The average American eats out 190 times per year! But most restaurant food is not nutritionally balanced. We try to correct this by eating a salad or a vegetable before we go or taking cut-up garden tomatoes to cover our pizzas. We have also developed a preference for restaurants that serve Chinese food or homemade soups or a salad bar. (Note: a salad bar's fresh fruit, dark greens, and raw vegetables contain the most nutrients.)

Additionally, we combat poor eating habits by feeding our boys information. For example, we teach them how to read nutritional labels on food packages — the kinds of flour or oil, the number of additives, the amounts of sugar and salt, the calories, the caffeine. Or, when one of them asks, "Mom, why do I have to eat these yukky carrots," we give them more than a "because-it's-good-for-you." We explain that carrots provide vitamin A, a vitamin which may decrease the risk of lung or stomach cancer. As they learn how their diet effects their life span, energy, heart, and teeth, they will more assuredly adopt our values.

Finally — a word of caution. God designed meals for fellowship. Don't ruin His intent by forcing kids to eat unwanted foods or being overly picky about manners. Remember, the Romans and other Europeans had the habit of throwing their leftovers on the floor!

Conclusion

Throughout history, various diets have produced uniformly good health. From the Eskimos, who exist largely on marine animals, to the peoples of the tropics, who eat mainly rice and vegetables, "the human population [has] experienced approximately the same health standards."[23] Good nutrition, then, can be achieved through diverse diets. If we Americans select foods from the four basic food groups, with an accent on fruits, vegetables, and whole grains, we will be slimmer and healthier. But such simple advice is often ignored. On the other hand, if a nutritionist recommends that people eat ten pounds of stewed rhubarb without sugar every day, or that they may only have coffee if they put in salt and cider vinegar instead of sugar and milk, or that they must never eat eggs at the same meal as bacon, their dietary system will be in every women's magazine and Sunday supplement, and thousands of people will try it—for a day or so.[24]

Many of these strange diets emphasize a non-Biblical asceticism. Paul warned of false teachers who command people "to abstain from certain foods, which God created to be received with thanksgiving by those who believe and who know the truth. For everything God created is good, and nothing is to be rejected if it is received with thanksgiving" (1 Timothy 4:3–4). Any system of nutrition which emphasizes negatives should be rejected. Our bodies will not be horribly corrupted by an occasional candy bar or a greasy hamburger.

Children's Health: On Their Own

Children must learn self-care—unless we want to wipe the noses of our adult children! A forgotten ally in this process is experience. However, experience is a slow tutor and most parents want "Insty-Print" results. So we badger our kids, hoping to hurry their development. But if we are patient, natural circumstances will lend authority to our words. In our home, constipation helped a son recognize his need for more fruits and vegetables. A body rash—not nagging!—convinced a son to shower more frequently. The dentist drilled into our boys the need for dental hygiene.

Furthermore, in taking responsibility for his health, a child must understand his unique needs. For example:

- One of our boys is prone to a deep cough when he catches a cold. If not properly cared for, it can turn into bronchitis.

- Our middle son requires less sleep than his older brother — several months of difficulty in falling asleep revealed his need.

- Andrew is allergic to ragweed. He is learning that doing what is right and controlling his tongue are formidable tasks during the fall.

- Nathan has weak ankles that must be supported when he competes in some sports.

Additionally, self-care training must teach kids how to treat the common ailments — sprains, burns, cuts, colds, diarrhea, bruises. The home can be an effective transmitter of this information because it joins theory and practice. When Nathan's toe became infected, we directed him to the child medical encyclopedia. There he was instructed to soak his toe, to avoid putting pressure on it, and to look for red streaks (a sign of spreading infection). Nathan was motivated — by the pain in his toe! — to learn how to treat an infection.

Conclusion

Edith Schaeffer offers a model of caring for our children's health needs:

> For some people the memory of illness carries with it the memory of loving care, cool hands stroking the forehead, sponge baths in bed, clean sheets under a hot chin, lovely-flavored drinks, alcohol back rubs, medicine given methodically by the clock, flowers near the bed, curtains drawn when fever is hurting the eyes, soft singing of a mother's or father's voice during a sleepless night.[25]

The spirits of children can't be seen or handled. But we may touch their hearts deeply by nurturing their physical needs.

PART SIX

CONCLUSION

15

YOU CAN REMODEL
YOUR FAMILY

Will society return control of children to the family, where char-
acter can best be structured in relation to loving and at the
same time restraining parents? Can we return self-assurance to
mothers and fathers? . . . Or is it too late to stop the inexorable
movement led by professionals, justified by academics, funded
by the government, and publicized by the media, that claims
society knows best — and is ready to tell mothers and fathers
how to do it, and even do it for them?[1]

A mother's ponderings remind us of the radical changes in
our society:

The swings are empty. No one is on the slide or the Jun-
gle-Gym. My son runs across the grassy field, returns and
asks if I will share the seesaw. . . . We have lived in three
different communities in Alexander's five short years and it
has always been the same: he has no one to play with.

Where are the other children on this sunlit, sparkling afternoon? Can no other mothers or fathers steal away for an

hour in the park? I know the answers now. Many of the other children are in day-care. Most of the other parents are at work. Yet as I watch my son swing and then slide by himself, I am sad. . . .

Perhaps someday we will live someplace where it will be possible for him to play outside with other children without any prior planning. But right now, even on weekends and evenings when kids are back in their neighborhoods, they remain indoors. It is no longer safe for them to roam the neighborhood as I could when I was a child. Instead, they watch TV inside the temperature-controlled fortresses we call our homes.

I can't help but wonder if he will ever play kick-the-can in the gathering dusk of a chill autumn afternoon. Will he ever run so fast and far that his side aches, yet still dread my voice calling him in to supper? Will he ever roll down-hill in an old barrel or a dilapidated box? Will he ever, on impulse, stomp on frozen puddles of morning ice or play marbles until his hands are grimy and red with cold?[2]

Can the functions of the home be revived, or are they in inevitable decline? One critic of traditional values concluded: "Our research has convinced us that the chances for a large-scale restoration of these traditional values are near zero."[3] "Large-scale"? Size is not the issue.

The metaphors Jesus used . . . are frequently images of the single, the small, and the quiet, which have effects far in excess of their appearance: salt, leaven, seed. Our culture publicizes the opposite emphasis: the big, the multitudinous, the noisy.[4]

Obedience, not popularity, is the issue. But what is God calling families to do?

Reviewing the Need

Who Will Guide Our Children?

While browsing through a clothing sale with my eldest son, his heart became locked on a sixty dollar pair of tennis shoes. Inspite of my refusals to spend that much money, he continued to plead—"But Dad, we will save almost twenty dollars!" As I lay in bed that night, I was frustrated by my son's attitude and my inability to sway him. The next day I tried a new approach, explaining that we spend about $250 per year on his clothing. I then asked: "Would it be wise to spend more than twenty percent of the budget on one pair of shoes?" He immediately recognized that it would not. The next day we found a pair of shoes he liked better for less than half of the price.

Did I plan that shopping trip to be an economics lesson for my son? No. The lesson came because I spent the evening with him.

God's design for parents is to be on hand at those teachable moments: "When your son asks you, . . . tell him. . . ." (see Deuteronomy 6:20f). Availability is crucial because "children do not make notes about their questions to bring up at a more convenient time. They wonder about things according to the rhythm of their inner life, and ask whoever is there at the moment."[5] Because most parents are not available, children depend on their agemates for encouragement, advice, comfort. No wonder the teen suicide rate has tripled during the past twenty years. The immature cannot guide the immature. The blind cannot lead the blind.

Who Will Challenge
Our Children to Serve the King of Kings?

The faith of Paul's missionary companion, Timothy, was stirred by the models in his home. Paul said, "I have been reminded of your sincere faith, which first lived in your grandmother Lois and in your mother Eunice and, I am persuaded, now lives in you also" (2 Timothy 1:5). Similarly, Virginia Owens praised her mother who "blew prayers into [her] pitifully shrunken little destiny to keep it alive." This "immortal in disguise" challenged her with a heavenly vision: "Raised to believe in special purposes and high callings, I confronted a world where the best that was offered was a score on an aptitude test."[6]

We parents are commanded to "impress" and "talk about" God's truths to our children. We are told to bring up our children in "the training and instruction of the Lord." Children are warned: "Keep your father's commands and do not forsake your mother's teaching" (Proverbs 6:20). Scripture is clear: parents have the primary task in passing the faith onto the next generation.

Who Will Shelter Our Children?

The five-year-old daughter of a career-oriented woman unknowingly convinced her mom to become a homemaker.

> As we drove up the hill, she said matter-of-factly, "This is where I always cry a little on my way to the [day-care] center."
>
> "Oh?" I tried to sound as casual as I could so that she would keep talking.
>
> "Yes," she said, "I usually cry right at the top of the hill."
>
> "Why is that?"
>
> "Oh, just because I can't go home and you're not with me. I just want to go home after school."
>
> What Jenny said hit me hard partly because she told me in such an accepting, matter-of-fact voice. She was not being manipulative. She wanted to tell me her feelings.[7]

This little girl's desire to be home with her mom reflects a God-given need: to be surrounded by parental love — "When you sit at home and when you walk along the road, when you lie down and when you get up." As a child, an "I'm home, Mom!" was welcomed with a smile, and frequently, a freshly baked cookie. What would it have been like to be greeted by an empty house day after day after day? I shudder at the thought.

Who Will Shelter Our Adults?

Adults also need a sanctuary. God repeatedly told Israel to care for adults who had lost the shelter of their homes: "[God] defends the cause of the fatherless and the widow, and loves the alien, giving him food and clothing. And you are to love those who are aliens" (Deuteronomy 10:18–19).

If historian Page Smith's attitude toward his home was echoed by a majority of Americans, our society would be transformed: "I have spent as much of my life in [my home] as I could. I leave it reluctantly; I return to it joyfully. I can hardly persuade my wife to leave it at all." Smith concluded: "I have a settled conviction that a man's and a woman's place is in the home."[8]

Who Will Care for Our Handicapped or Our Aged?

Institutions are seldom the answer to the question of care for the handicapped and the aged.

Peggy is the mother of four healthy sons and a daughter with Down's syndrome. Back when Jennifer was born, doctors were still telling mothers to put their Down's syndrome babies in an institution because they were "bound to be vegetables for life." Disregarding this august advice, Peggy began developing her own therapy program for Jennifer. Jennifer is now in the sixth grade in a "normal" classroom at the age of thirteen, can read and write, and leads her class in Bible memory work! Peggy's mother also lives with her, confined to a wheelchair from which Peggy must lift her to her bed, to the toilet, to her chair, and so on. Peggy is active in her church, extends hospitality to all who show the slightest signs of needing it . . . and is the ever-willing grandmother of a flock of beautiful young girls.[9]

Scripture warns us: "If anyone does not provide for his relatives, and especially for his immediate family, he has denied the faith and is worse than an unbeliever" (1 Timothy 5:8).

Some children dismiss the thought of housing an aging parent, believing their jobs are too demanding. Might God direct them to quit or change their jobs? Some people excuse themselves from sheltering a dying relative, citing their inexperience in health care. Could God teach them how to nurse the dying? Mary Pride explained why the Francis Schaeffer family brought Francis home to die:

> Dr. Schaeffer, like so many of us, didn't want to die in a noisy, neon-lit intensive care unit, sedated to the point of imbecility. He got his wish. The family made up a bed for him in the living room, where he could look out the front window and see the sky, and nursed him themselves in his last days. He died right there, in front of his own fireplace, in the arms of his wife.[10]

The choices are seldom easy or clear. But we must search out and perform our God-directed responsibility.

Remembering the Costs

Remodeling the home is costly. Prior to becoming a homemaker, Cathy worked in a campus ministry. Her days were spent advising students, leading Bible studies, speaking in classrooms. When our first child was born, she chose to give up many of those tasks, to give herself to our infant son.

But moms can't be expected to pay the whole bill. I also limit my commitments outside the home so that I can direct my sons' education, coach their athletic teams, and lead family worship.

Furthermore, there may be a literal cost in renewing your home. A woman's decision to become a full-time homemaker came at a point when the couple had just become debt free, and looked forward to living well,

> eating out more often, having a "real" summer vacation at a resort, getting someone in to clean several hours a week, and giving the children a lot more materially and culturally. The idea of living well was very tempting. But we decided instead to opt for an emotional luxury. It was, however — and still is — difficult to be surrounded by a society full of exciting things and opportunities and to do without most of them.[11]

Reaping the Rewards

God declares that fulfillment comes through service — "whoever wants to become great among you must be your servant" (Matthew 20:26). One mother explained her joy in caring for a newborn:

> Things that at first bothered me, like having milk burp-ups on the shoulder of my blouses, didn't seem particularly important after a while. I got into perspective what really mattered to me. Spending the day loving a small person seemed a pretty impressive way to live to me. I found motherhood an involving, exhausting, stimulating job.[12]

Some of the rewards may come from unexpected sources. A child with a working mother remembered the homes of her friends:

> Those stay-at-home mothers profoundly influenced my young life. One, who was pregnant with her third child, allowed me to feel her swollen abdomen and taught me

about the joy of childbirth. Another, a fine pianist, not only filled my untutored ears with the sound of classical music but she and her daughter were emotionally close. As I watched their interaction, I saw an intimacy that my mother and I did not share, and this mother-daughter relationship touched a longing too deep for words.

When I became an adolescent, another neighbor introduced me to Christianity. Martha was a follower of Jesus, a Jesus so real that He paid her rent and food bill when her husband, an alcoholic, disappeared for periods of time. As I watched this strong, joyful woman rise above the wretchedness of her circumstances, I too wanted to know this Jesus. Gradually He became a reality to me, and in the process I became Martha's "child of the spirit," or so she called me.[13]

Seldom is work outside the home more fulfilling than introducing teens to the richness of family life or to the Savior.

Remodeling Your Home

Every family approaches these truths with varying problems and potentials:

No one gets a clean, blank slate on which to scrawl his message to the world; it is already dusty with chalk and scribbled with markings from the past. But we all have to start somewhere. We all have to have an earthen vessel, inherited, common as clay, whose design we had no control over. We all have a place, particular and limited, . . . from which to set out.[14]

The pace and extent of change in each home will vary. But a long journey is accomplished a step at a time.

A millionaire was interviewed: "Tell me, sir, how did you manage to amass such a fortune?" He shrugged his shoulders and confessed: "I really don't know. I just woke up one morning and found that my bank account had tons of money in it." Likely story? Hardly. A person does not become a millionaire without a plan of action.

Similarly, a "million dollar" family won't be achieved without planning. Take a sabbatical from volunteer work to read, pray, and get direction from God. Otherwise, the cries of the world will drown out the "gentle whisper" of God.

Not only does remodeling the home take planning, but also perseverance. The author of Hebrews informs us that we must "run with *perseverance* the race marked out for us" (Hebrews 12:1, emphasis added). Paul warns us not to give up doing good because "at the proper time we will reap a harvest *if we do not give up*" (Galatians 6:9, emphasis added). Similarly, Edith Schaeffer observed:

All the admirable things written about [the wife in Proverbs 31] did not take place in one year. It seems to me it is a summary of the great diversity of accomplishments and the results of her work and imagination and talents over a long period of time. . . .

The description of this woman getting up while it is dark to prepare interesting food for her family, and working with eager hands to spin and weave flax, is a picture of something that has had continuity, something that has taken place over a long period of time. Flax has had time to grow, to be harvested, to be spun, to be woven into cloth, to be made into an amazing array of things. We are not being told about a short spurt of energy and imagination which soon turns to another man, or to another career after a minimal trial![15]

The rewards from a commitment to our homes are great — to those who labor day-by-day, week-by-week, year-by-year.

As I have reread and edited this book, I am humbled by my family's lowly application of these lofty principles. Our kids are not always willing workers. They frequently lash at each other with their tongues. They battle bitterly over such life-and-death issues as who will take the first bath. On our side, seldom a day goes by that Cathy and I don't fling unjust accusations or rage over trivialities. But we don't give up — because we believe that family constitutes "most of what matters about human life. All the rest — all the going and coming, getting and spending, building and breaking and building again — are probably the lesser part, even though they apparently dominate our days."[16]

Supporting the Revival of the Family

But the burden for this renewal must be shared. Cathy and I anticipate the day our children will leave our household. But that isn't the time to crawl into a shell of privacy. We look forward to supporting younger families committed to a Biblical style of family life.

Churches have sometimes undermined the enrichment of homes by keeping families overly busy and by focusing their assistance on families of working mothers (e.g., through day-care services). Furthermore, they often expect full-time homemakers to shoulder the volunteer burden in the church.

However, churches can be the leaders in restoring family life. Our church has begun a "Moms' Morning Out." Young homemakers are treated to a morning of Bible study and free-time while volunteers watch their children.

Churches can also encourage more intimate ties within families by challenging them to minister as a unit — reaching out to neighborhood kids, visiting shut-ins, adopting missionaries, caring for the church grounds.

Finally, the church can help broken or dislocated families by finding substitute grandparents for the kids. Children need a diversity of mature models in their lives.

Time and Choices

Edith Schaeffer knew a grandmother who cared for her grandchildren while her daughter nurtured a career. This grandmother gave sacrificially of her time and energy but was unappreciated. Her daughter "turned against her with a rather ugly bitterness. Why? Because the love of the children has turned to the grandmother. Their secrets and longings are shared with her. They ask for their grandmother at moments of fear or special need. The mother is suddenly waking up to the fact that she has not simply lost love and relationship, but time."[17]

One day follows another. Time flows. Springtime planting precedes autumn harvest. Autumn's freezing of vegetables and making of jellies and jam precedes eating that food in front of a roaring fire as the snow blows against windows in the winter's storms.

. . . To forget that if the seeds are not planted and weeded and watered, there will be nothing but wilderness at harvest time is the same as forgetting that the richness of growing relationships . . . may be experienced only through *time* and *choice*. . . . There is no possibility of having loving grandchildren to keep one alive and young if the choice has not been made to use life earlier for continuity of planting, weeding, watering, and caring for the relationships. There is a moment when "too late" is an agonizing realization! *Life's time has been spent in that which has provided nothing at all for the winter's blast.*[17]

Parents, the years flee by. It seems just yesterday that we joyously celebrated the birth of our first son. Within three years he will probably give up permanent residence in our home. What choices are you making?

See, I set before you today life and prosperity, death and destruction. For I command you today to love the LORD your God, to walk in his ways, and to keep his commands,

decrees and laws; then you will live and increase, and the LORD your God will bless you in the land you are entering to possess.

But if your heart turns away and you are not obedient, and if you are drawn away to bow down to other gods and worship them, I declare to you this day that you will certainly be destroyed. (Deuteronomy 30:15–18)

What will you choose? Life or death? God or the gods of this world? May God give you the grace, wisdom, and strength to choose His model for your family.

END NOTES

INTRODUCTION

1. Arthur Kornhaber and Kenneth L. Woodward, *Grandparents/Grandchildren: The Vital Connection* (Garden City, New York: Anchor Press/Doubleday, 1981), 157.
2. *Eerdmans' Handbook to Christianity in America* (Grand Rapids, MI: W.B. Eerdmans Co., 1983), 84.
3. Virginia Tufte and Barbara Myerhoff, *Changing Images of the Family* (New Haven: Yale University Press, 1979), 226.
4. "Adult Kids Are Filling Empty Nests," *Sioux Scene*, January 27, 1988, 1.
5. "News," *Focus on the Family Magazine*, August, 1987, 11.
6. Daniel Boorstin, "The Twin Menaces: Illiteracy, Aliteracy," *USA Today*, December 12, 1984.
7. Marie Winn, *Children Without Childhood* (New York: Pantheon Books, 1981), 124.
8. Norma Peterson, "Teenage Apathy, Epidemic of the 80's," *USA Today*, November 8, 1983.
9. "High-Achieving Teenagers Admit Cheating," *Sioux Falls Argus Leader*, November 1, 1983.
10. David Elkind, *All Grown Up and No Place to Go: Teenagers in Crisis* (Reading, MA: Addison-Wesley Publishing Company, 1984), 7.
11. Allan Bloom, *The Closing of the American Mind* (New York: Simon and Schuster, 1987), 22.
12. Virginia Stem Owens, *A Feast of Families* (Grand Rapids: Zondervan, 1983), 24.
13. Bloom, 127.

CHAPTER 1: THE TRANSFORMATION OF SCHOOLS

1. Robert Marquand, "Textbooks: Debate Heats Up Over the Growing Push for Reform," *Christian Science Monitor*, October 25, 1985.
2. "What the Teachers Say," *USA Today*, October 3, 1983.
3. John Goodlad, *A Place Called School* (New York: McGraw-Hill Book Company, 1984), 77.
4. Pat Ordovensky, "SATs Up 9, 'Education on Mend,'" *USA Today*, October 24, 1985.
5. David Nasaw, *Schooled to Order: A Social History of Public Schooling in the United States* (New York: Oxford University Press, 1979), 61.
6. David Tyack and Elisabeth Hansot, *Managers of Virtue: Public School Leadership in America, 1820–1980* (New York: Basic Books, 1984), 105.
7. Page Smith, *The Rise of Industrial America* (New York: McGraw-Hill Book Co., 1984), 587.
8. Goodlad, 15.
9. H. Warren Button and Eugene Provenzo, Jr., *History of Education and Culture in America* (Englewood Cliffs: Prentice-Hall, Inc., 1983), 122.
10. W.R. Wees, *Nobody Can Teach Anyone Anything* (Toronto: Doubleday Canada Limited, 1971), 16.
11. Jerome Kagan, *The Nature of the Child* (New York: Basic Books, 1984), 273.
12. Kim Painter, "Troubled Teens Turn to Music, Not Mom," *USA Today*, October 30, 1986.
13. John Holt, *Teach Your Own: A Hopeful Path for Education* (New York: Dell Books, 1981), 73.
14. Tyack and Hansot, 205.
15. Marquand.
16. Goodlad, 48.
17. Marquand.
18. Jonathan Kozol, *On Being a Teacher* (New York: Continuum, 1981), 17.
19. Tyack and Hansot, 17.
20. Seymour Sarason, *Schooling in America: Scapegoat and Salvation* (New York: Free Press, 1983), 107.
21. Tyack and Hansot, 249.

CHAPTER 2: THE LIABILITIES OF FORMAL SCHOOLING

1. Goodlad, 108.
2. Ernest Boyer, *Highschool: A Report on Secondary Education in America* (New York: Harper and Row, 1984), 79.
3. "Harvard Accepts Home-Taught Student," *Sioux Falls Argus Leader*, August 8, 1983.
4. "Science Students High Scorers," *USA Today*, October 24, 1985.
5. Sue Radosti, Private letter.
6. Emily Feistritzer, "Consultant: Close Down Half the Nation's Teacher Training Programs," *Sioux Falls Argus Leader*, August 29, 1984.
7. Boyer, 159.
8. Neil Postman and Charles Weingartner, *Teaching as a Subversive Activity* (New York: Dell Publishing Co., 1969), xiii.
9. Bloom, 59.
10. Eda LeShan, *The Conspiracy Against Childhood* (New York: Atheneum, 1971), 149.
11. Goodlad, 109.
12. Wees, 47.
13. Ibid., 97.
14. "A Different Sort of Sport," *Newsweek*, July 2, 1984, 72.
15. Paula Skreslet, "The Prizes of First Grade," *Newsweek*, November 30, 1987, 8.
16. Ibid.
17. John Holt, *How Kids Fail*, (New York: Pitman Publishing Corporation, 1964), 38-39.
18. Goodlad, 77.
19. LeShan, 220.
20. Peter Brimelow, "Are We Spending Too Much on Education?" *Forbes*, December 29, 1986, 72.
21. Pat Ordovensky, "Defect Rate 50% from USA Schools," *USA Today*, October 27, 1987.

CHAPTER 3: HOME-CENTERED SCHOOLING

1. Bloom, 58.
2. David Elkind, *The Hurried Child* (Reading, MA: Addison-Wesley Publishing Co., 1981), 54.
3. Diane Ravitch, *The Schools We Deserve* (New York: Basic Books, 1985), 115.

4. Sarason, 123.
5. Larry Arnoldsen, "Professor Interested in Home Education," *Family Report*, January/February 1988, 3.
6. Wees, 67.
7. Arnoldsen.
8. Marquand.
9. Sarason, 137.
10. Ravitch, 76f.
11. Goodlad, 107.
12. Nancie Atwell, "How We Learned to Write," *Learning*, March, 1985, 51.
13. Sarason, 113.
14. Elkind, *The Hurried Child*, 65f.
15. Jon Walker, "Educator: Schools Waste Much Classroom Time," *Sioux Falls Argus Leader*, February 22, 1985.
16. Raymond and Dorothy Moore, *Home Grown Kids* (Waco, TX: Word Books, 1981), 39.
17. Marie Winn, *Children Without Childhood* (New York: Pantheon Books, 1981), 24.
18. Barbara Zigli, "Moms Affect Schoolwork," *USA Today*, April 26, 1984.
19. Pat Ordovensky, "Junior High: It's a Downer," *USA Today*, January 1, 1987.
20. Goodlad, 36.
21. Brenda Hunter, *Where Have All the Mothers Gone?* (Grand Rapids: Zondervan, 1982), 15.
22. Stephen Clark, *Man and Woman in Christ* (Ann Arbor: Servant Books, 1980), 68.

CHAPTER 4: THE TRANSFORMATION OF WORK

1. Robert Bellah, Richard Madsen, William Sullivan, Ann Swidler, and Steven Tipton, *Habits of the Heart* (Berkeley: University of California, 1985), 66.
2. Ibid., 72.
3. Ibid., 22.
4. "Interview with Gordon McDonald," *Christianity Today*, July 10, 1985, 38.
5. Tufte and Myerhoff, 51–52.
6. Ibid., 53.

7. Ruth Cowan, *More Work for Mother* (New York: Basic Books, 1983), 187f.
8. Christine Davidson, *Staying Home Instead* (Lexington, MA: Lexington Books, 1986), 23.
9. Ibid., 10.
10. Viviana Zelizer, *Pricing the Priceless Child* (New York: Basic Books, 1985), 11.
11. Ibid.
12. Ibid.
13. John and Virginia Demos, "Adolescence in Historical Perspective," in *The American Family in Social-Historical Perspective*, ed., Michael Gordon (New York: St. Martin's Press, 1973), 213.
14. Bloom, 128.
15. Hunter, 25f.
16. Alvin Toffler, *The Third Wave* (New York: Morrow Publishing, 1980), 66.
17. E. F. Schumacher, *Good Work* (New York: Harper and Row, 1979), 27.
18. Leo Tolstoy, *Anna Karenina* (New York: Bantam Books, 1960), 343.
19. William McConnell, *The Gift of Time* (Downers Grove, IL: InterVarsity Press, 1983), 37.
20. Edith Schaeffer, *What Is a Family?* (Old Tappan, NJ: Fleming H. Revell Co., 1975), 162.

CHAPTER 5: BRINGING WORK HOME

1. Kornhaber and Woodward, 151.
2. Mark Gerzon, *A Choice of Heroes: The Changing Face of American Manhood* (Boston: Houghton Mifflin Company, 1982), 126f.
3. Michael Hall, *The Last American Puritan: The Life of Increase Mather* (Middletown, Connecticut: Wesleyan University Press, 1988), 21.
4. Maggie Felser, "How Fares Superwoman?," *Minneapolis Tribune*, May 24, 1987.
5. Durmeriss Cruver, "Husbands and Housework: It's Still an Uneven Load," *USA Today*, August 20, 1986.
6. Davidson, 11.
7. Wally Metts, Jr., "Home-Grown Kids Need a Full-Time Mom," *Christianity Today*, March 6, 1987, 12.
8. Zelizer, 208–225.

9. H. Mussen, J.J. Conger, and J. Kagan, *Child Development and Personality* (New York: Harper and Row, 1974), 434–436.
10. Robert Banks, *The Tyranny of Time* (Downers Grove, IL: InterVarsity Press, 1983), 77.

CHAPTER 6: FAMILY WORK: GETTING YOUR HANDS DIRTY

1. Scott Burns, *The Household Economy* (Boston: Beacon Press, 1975), 63.
2. Ibid.
3. John Schwartz and Dody Tsiantar, "Escape from the Office," *Newsweek*, April 24, 1989, 58f.
4. Wesley Granberg-Michaelson, *A Worldly Spirituality* (New York: Harper and Row, 1985), 81.
5. David Shi, *The Simple Life: Plain Living and High Thinking in American Culture* (New York: Oxford University Press, 1985), 279.
6. Ibid., 277.
7. Eliot Daley, *Father Feelings* (New York: William Morrow and Company, 1978), 48.
8. Rhonda Sharp, "Straight Talk from the Sitter," *Newsweek*, July 18, 1988, 10.
9. Shirley Radl, *How to Be a Mother—and a Person, Too* (New York: Rawson, Wade Publishers, 1979), 169.
10. Gerzon, 212.

CHAPTER 7: CHILDREN AND WORK

1. Bernard Goldstein and Jack Oldham, *Children and Work: A Study of Socialization* (New Brunswick, New Jersey: Transaction Books, 1979), 119.
2. John Stott, *Involvement: Social and Sexual Relationships in the Modern World* (Old Tappan, New Jersey: Fleming H. Revell, 1984), 27f.
3. Ibid., 29.
4. Zelizer, 209.
5. Ellen Greenberger and Laurence Steinberg, *When Teenagers Work: The Psychological and Social Costs of Adolescent Employment* (New York: Basic Books, 1986).
6. Ibid., 11.
7. Ibid., 82.
8. Ibid., 85.

9. Ibid., 100.
10. Ibid., 223.
11. Sarason, 76.
12. Greenberger and Steinberg, 221.
13. Sarason, 122.
14. John Heimann, "'Daddy, What Do You Do?,'" *Newsweek*, January 4, 1989, 8.
15. Ibid.
16. Holt, *Teach Your Own*, 258.
17. Ibid.

CHAPTER 8: SOCIALIZATION: THE LOSS OF COMMUNITY

1. Owens, 14.
2. Madeleine L'Engle, *The Weather of the Heart* (Wheaton, IL: Harold Shaw Publishers, 1978), 13.
3. Painter.
4. Kornhaber and Woodward, 111f.
5. Mary Ann Delmonico Kuharski, "A Love of Family Affairs," *Newsweek*, August 21, 1989, 8.
6. Kornhaber and Woodward, 123f.
7. Bellah, et al., 142.
8. Tufte and Myerhoff, 71.
9. Michael Schudson, *Advertising, the Uneasy Persuasion* (New York: Basic Books, 1984), 153f.
10. Timothy Brubaker, *Family Relationships in Later Life* (London: Sage Publications, 1983), 64.
11. Carol Kuykendall, *Learning to Let Go* (Grand Rapids: Zondervan, 1985), 12.
12. Ibid., 7.
13. Ibid., 24.
14. "NW Bell Establishes Chatter Line," *Sioux Falls Argus Leader*, October 16, 1985.
15. Bellah, et al., 23.
16. Daniel Boorstin, *The Americans: The Democratic Experience* (New York: Vintage Books, 1973), 104.
17. Ibid., 136.
18. Neil Postman, *Amusing Ourselves to Death: Public Discourse in the Age of Show Business* (New York: Viking Press, 1985), 47.
19. Kornhaber and Woodward, 136.

CHAPTER 9: RESTORING COMMUNITY: THE IMMEDIATE FAMILY

1. Rita Kramer, *In Defense of the Family* (New York: Basic Books, 1983), 128.
2. Winn, 192.
3. Owens, 15.
4. Gail Sheehy, *Passages: Predictable Crises of Adult Life* (New York: Bantam Books, 1977), 364.
5. Winn, 5f.
6. Ibid.
7. Daley, 96.
8. Winn, 3.
9. Elkind, *The Hurried Child*, 83.
10. Winn, 45.
11. Bloom, 68.
12. Ibid., 75.
13. Mussen, Conger, and Kagan, 577.
14. David Perry and Kay Bussey, *Social Development* (Englewood Cliffs, NJ: Prentice-Hall, Inc., 1984), 64f.
15. Mussen, Conger, and Kagan, 577.
16. Urie Bronfenbrenner, *Two Worlds of Childhood: U.S. and U.S.S.R.* (New York: Simon and Schuster, 1970), 116f.
17. Hunter, 31.
18. Winn, 198.
19. Ibid., 199.
20. Kramer, 99.
21. Daley, 32.
22. Madeleine L'Engle, *The Summer of the Great-Grandmother* (New York: Seabury Press, 1979), 28.
23. Fitzhugh Dodson, *How to Grand-Parent* (New York: Plume Books, 1981), 3f.
24. Alvin Rogness, *The Word for Every Day* (Minneapolis: Augsburg Publishing, 1981), 49.

CHAPTER 10: RESTORING COMMUNITY: THE EXTENDED FAMILY

1. Kuharski.
2. Ibid., 23.
3. Ibid., 131.

4. Ibid., 14.
5. Ibid., 41f.
6. Wees, 86.
7. Andrew Cherlin and Frank Furstenberg, Jr., *The New American Grandparent* (New York: Basic Books, 1986), 29–33.
8. Brubaker, 63f.
9. Cherlin and Furstenberg, 10.
10. Dodson, 4.
11. Kornhaber and Woodward, 119.
12. Dodson, 21.
13. Owens, 20.
14. Kornhaber and Woodward, 204.
15. Tim Keller, "Anything Do Us Part," *Eternity*, June, 1987, 22.
16. Gail Baruch, "Virginity Topic of Teen Magazine," *Sioux Scene*, April 20, 1988.
17. Daley, 13.

CHAPTER 11: LAYING THE FOUNDATION

1. Elkind, *The Hurried Child*, 81.
2. C. B. Eavey, *History of Christian Education* (Chicago: Moody Press, 1964), 191.
3. "Learning About Sex," *USA Today*, October 26, 1985.
4. Donald Wildmon, *The Home Invaders* (Wheaton, IL: Victor Books, 1985), 109.
5. D. Ng and V. Thomas, *Children in the Worshipping Community* (Atlanta: John Knox Press, 1981), 67.
6. McConnell, 28.
7. Banks, 70.

CHAPTER 12: PASSING ON THE FAITH

1. Bloom, 57.
2. Owens, 61f.
3. Bloom, 57.
4. Hall, 41.
5. Owens, 97.
6. McConnell, 61f.
7. Norman Wakefield, "Children and Their Theological Concepts," in *Childhood Education in the Church*, eds. R. Zuck and R. Clark (Chicago: Moody Press, 1975), 119–133.

8. Hunter, 52.
9. Daley, 91.
10. Kornhaber and Woodward, 45.

CHAPTER 13: LEISURE IN THE HOME

1. Tim Hansel, *When I Relax I Feel Guilty* (Elgin, IL: David C. Cook Publishing Co., 1979), 30.
2. Banks, 80.
3. Sebastian De Grazia, *Of Time, Work, and Leisure* (Garden City, NY: Anchor Books, 1962), 108.
4. Ibid.
5. Tyack and Hansot, 27.
6. Richard Foster, *Celebration of Discipline* (New York: Harper and Row, 1978), 20f.
7. Author unknown, quoted in Hansel, 67.
8. LeShan, 327.
9. Banks, 191.
10. Eugene Peterson, "The Unbusy Pastor," *Leadership*, Summer, 1981, 71.
11. Ibid.
12. Ibid., 70.
13. Daley, 113.
14. Ibid., 47.
15. Ibid., 103.
16. Ibid., 166.

CHAPTER 14: FAMILY HEALTH

1. Quoted by Terence McLaughlin, *If You Like It, Don't Eat It: Dietary Fads and Fancies* (New York: Universe Books, 1979), 90.
2. "What Do We Really Know?", University of California, *Berkeley Wellness Letter*, Vol. 4, No. 5, February, 1988.
3. Martin Marty, "The Entertwining of Religion and Health/Medicine in Culture," in *Health/Medicine and the Faith Traditions*, Martin Marty and Kenneth Vaux, eds., (Philadelphia: Fortress Press, 1982), 27.
4. Kirkpatrick Sale, *Human Scale* (New York: Coward, McCann and Geoghegan, 1980), 270.
5. Robert Mendelsohn, *How to Raise a Healthy Child . . . In Spite of Your Doctor* (Chicago: Contemporary Books, Inc., 1984), 7.

6. "Medical Students Forget Nutrition," *Sioux Falls Argus Leader,* January 3, 1989.

7. Stephen Hoffmann, "The Doctor as Dramatist," *Newsweek,* February 1, 1988, 10.

8. Sale, 267.

9. John Pleas, *Walking* (New York: W.W. Norton and Co., 1982), 15.

10. "The Fit Body," University of California, *Berkeley Wellness Letter,* Vol.5, No.5, February 1989.

11. Pleas, 106.

12. "Exercise and Heart Disease: The Smoking Gun," University of California, *Berkeley Wellness Letter,* Vol.4, No.1, October 1987.

13. James Rippe, "For a Lifelong Healthy Heart: Choose Exercise," *Newsweek,* February 13, 1989.

14. "News," *Focus on the Family,* August, 1987, 11.

15. McLaughlin, 31.

16. W.H. LeRiche, *A Chemical Feast* (New York: Facts on File Publications, 1982), 21.

17. Quoted in McLaughlin, 11.

18. "Fresh, Frozen, or Canned," *Berkeley Wellness Letter,* Vol. 4, No. 1, 7.

19. "Late-Night Eating Gets the OK," *Health,* January, 1989, 16.

20. LeRiche, 29.

21. "Dangers of Pesticides Hurt Benefits of Fruit, Vegetables," *Sioux Falls Argus Leader,* May 4, 1988.

22. Timothy Johnson and Stephen Goldfinger, eds., *The Harvard Medical School Health Letter Book* (Cambridge, MA: Harvard University Press, 1981), 23.

23. Elmer McCollum, *A History of Nutrition* (Boston: Houghton Mifflin Co., 1965), 1.

24. McLaughlin, 73.

25. Schaeffer, *What Is a Family?,* 94.

CHAPTER 15: YOU CAN REMODEL YOUR HOME

1. Kramer, 21.

2. Phyllis Hall, "All Our Lonely Children," *Newsweek,* October 12, 1987, 12.

3. Cherlin and Furstenberg, 190.

4. Peterson, 71.

5. Kramer, 87.

6. Owens, 61–64.
7. Davidson, 4.
8. Page Smith, *Dissenting Opinions* (San Francisco: North Point Press, 1984), 168.
9. Mary Pride, *The Way Home: Beyond Feminism, Back to Reality* (Westchester, IL: Crossway Books, 1985), 192f.
10. Ibid.
11. Davidson, 8.
12. Ibid., 18.
13. Hunter, 29.
14. Owens, 84.
15. Edith Schaeffer, *Common Sense Christian Living* (Nashville: Thomas Nelson Publishers, 1983), 108f.
16. Daley, 7f.
17. Schaeffer, *Common Sense Christian Living*, 106.
18. Ibid.

ABOUT THE AUTHOR

D r. Bernie Schock lives in Sioux Falls, South Dakota with his wife, Cathy, and their three sons — Nathan, Andrew, and Jered. Bernie writes, teaches part-time at a Christian College, serves as president for the South Dakota Home School Association, and supervises a family lawn-care service.

This is his second book. The first one was *Parents, Kids, and Sports*, published by Moody Press. Bernie has degrees from Southern Methodist University (B.A.), Dallas Seminary (Th.M.), and the University of South Dakota (Ed.D).

The typeface for the text of this book is *Goudy Old Style*. Its creator, Frederic W. Goudy, was commissioned by American Type Founders Company to design a new Roman type face. Completed in 1915 and named Goudy Old Style, it was an instant bestseller. However, its designer had sold the design outright to the foundry, so when it became evident that additional versions would be needed to complete the family, the work was done by the foundry's own designer, Morris Benton. From the original design came seven additional weights and variants, all of which sold in great quantity. However, Goudy himself received no additional compensation for them. He later recounted a visit to the foundry with a group of printers, during which the guide stopped at one of the busy casting machines and stated, "Here's where Goudy goes down to posterity, while American Type Founders Company goes down to prosperity."

Substantive Editing:
Michael S. Hyatt

Copy Editing:
Susan Kirby

Cover Design:
Kent Puckett Associates, Atlanta, Georgia

Page Composition:
Xerox Ventura Publisher
Printware 720 IQ Laser Printer

Printing and Binding:
Maple-Vail Book Manufacturing Group,
York, Pennsylvania

Dust Jacket Printing:
Weber Graphics, Chicago, Illinois